Walter Schenck Presents

Euripides'

STAGE PLAYS COLLECTION

ELECTRA, ORESTES,
HELEN, THE PHOENICIAN VIRGINS

Translated By

Theodore Alois Buckley

VOL 3

Walter Joseph Schenck, Jr.

30

Euripides

Euripides, son of Cleito and Mnesarchus, was born in 480 B.C.E. on Salamis Island, Greece and died in 406 B.C.E. in Macedonia. Medea was written 431 B.C.E

Theodore Alois Buckley

Rev. Theodore Alois Buckley was a translator of classical plays and literature. He was an opium addict and an alcoholic. He was born in 1825 and died in 1856.

Walter Joseph Schenck, Jr.

Walter was born on May 7, 1950 in Warrensburg, MO, and currently lives in Jacksonville, FL. Walter is a professional member of the Dramatists Guild of America.

Reference Materials

The following public domain reference books are personally owned by Walter Joseph Schenck, Jr.

The Tragedies of Euripides, Literally Translated or Revised with Critical and Explanatory Notes, by Theodore Alois Buckley, of Christ Church. Vol. I. New York: Harper & Brothers, Publishers, Franklin Square. 1857.

The Tragedies of Euripides, Literally Translated or Revised with Critical and Explanatory Notes, by Theodore Alois Buckley, of Christ Church. Vol. II. New York: Harper & Brothers, Publishers, Franklin Square. 1857.

Additional Materials

Schenck's Official Stage Play Formatting Series: Vol. 67
Euripides' ELECTRA: Six Versions

Schenck's Official Stage Play Formatting Series: Vol. 68
Euripides' ORESTES: Five Versions

Schenck's Official Stage Play Formatting Series: Vol. 70
Euripides' HELEN: Five Versions

Schenck's Official Stage Play Formatting Series: Vol. 55
Euripides' PHOENICIAN MAIDENS: Five Versions

CONTENTS

ELECTRA

PERSONS REPRESENTED

PEASANT

ELECTRA

ORESTES

PYLADES (A dumb personage)

CHORUS

CLYTEMNESTRA

OLD MAN

MESSENGER

CASTOR AND POLLUX

THE ARGUMENT

The return of Orestes from exile, and his revenge upon Clyaemnestra and Aegisthus for the murder of Agamemnon. The subject is the same as that of the "Choephorae" of Aeschylus, and the " Electra" of Sophocles, but is handled with much less dramatic skill, while the development is tedious and inartistic.

PEASANT

O ancient Argos of the land, (and) ye streams of Inachus, whence once on a time king Agamemnon, conducting the war, in a thousand ships sailed to the Trojan land. And having slain Priam, the ruler over the Trojan land, and taken the renowned city of Dardanus, he came back to this Argos, and in the lofty temples placed very many spoils of the barbarians; and there indeed he was prosperous; but at home he perishes by stratagem at the hands of his wife Clytemnestra, and by the hand of Aegisthus, son of Thyestes. And he indeed, having left the ancient sceptre of Tantalus, is no more; but Aegisthus reigns over the land, having his wife, the daughter of Tyndarus. But they whom he left in his dwelling when he sailed to Troy, the male Orestes, and the female blossom of Electra, the former the old guardian of his father stole away, when, (by name) Orestes, he was about to perish by the hand of Aegisthus, and gave him to Strophius to train up in the land of the Phocians. But the latter (Electra) remained in the house of her father. Her, as soon as the blooming season of youth arrived, the first men of the land of Greece wooed as suitors. But fearing lest she should bring forth to any of the chieftains a son, who might take vengeance for Agamemnon, Aegisthus kept her in his house, nor united her to any bridegroom. But since this matter also was fraught with much dread, lest she should privily bear children to any noble man, when he wished to slay her, her mother, though cruel-minded, yet saved her from the hand of Aegisthus. For in regard to her husband's death she had a pretence; but she feared that by the death of her children she herself might die. [27]

Upon this, then, Aegisthus devised such a contrivance. He mentioned a sum of gold for him who should slay Orestes; who indeed was away from the land in exile; but to me he gives Electra to have as a wife, I being born of Mycenian sires; (and on this account, indeed, I am not liable to reproach, for I am noble at least in race, but yet poor in means, from whence a noble descent is lost;) that giving her to a humble person, he might have little fear. For if a man possessing dignity had obtained her, he would have roused up the death of Agamemnon, that now sleeps, and justice would then have come upon Aegisthus. But never did this man (Venus is my witness!) dishonor her in his bed, but she is still a virgin. For I am ashamed at having received the child of a prosperous family, to do her an insult, not being by birth worthy (of her). But I bewail the wretched Orestes, who is nominally related to me, if ever, returning to Argos, he shall behold the unhappy nuptials of his sister. But whoever says that I am foolish, because, having received a young virgin into my house, I touch her not, let him know that he measures continence by a bad rule of sentiment, and that he himself is such an one.   47

ELECTRA

O sable night, nurse of golden stars, during which, bearing this vessel placed on my head, I go in quest of river water; not indeed because I am reduced to so great necessity, but that I may show to the Gods the insult of Aegisthus, and may utter lamentations to the mighty ether for my sire. For the all-destructive daughter of Tyndarus, my mother, has cast me out of her house, doing a favor to her husband; and having borne other children to Aegisthus, she accounts Orestes and me as things unimportant in her house.   55

PEASANT

But why, O hapless one, dost thou labor thus for my sake, submitting to toils, when thou before wast well brought up, nor ceasest this, when I entreat you?   57

ELECTRA

I deem thee a friend equal to the Gods; for in mine ills thou hast not behaved insolently. But it is a great good fortune for mortals to find a physician in an evil calamity, as I obtain thee. It behooves me then, even unbidden, lightening thy toil to the utmost of my power, that thou mayest more easily bear it, to partake in thy labors. And thou hast work enough without; but matters within doors it behooves me to make ready. For it is sweet for a laborer entering from without, to find things within (his house) aright.   66

PEASANT

If indeed it seems fit to thee, go, for the streams are not far from this house. But I at dawn of day will drive my steers into the corn-lands, and sow the fields. For no slothful man, having the Gods continually in his mouth, will be able to obtain a livelihood without labor.   71

ORESTES

Pylades, for thee indeed I above all men account a faithful friend and guest to me; and thou alone of my friends hast respected me, Orestes, faring as I fare, having suffered terribly at the hands of Aegisthus, who, with my all-abandoned mother, destroyed my sire. But I have come from the oracles of the God to the Argive threshold, no one being conscious, in order to punish the slaughter of my father by slaughter.

But during this night having gone to the tomb of my sire, I both gave tears, and made offerings of my hair, and sacrificed at the tomb the blood of a slain sheep, unknown to the tyrants who sway this land. And within the walls, indeed, I advance not my foot; but I came to the boundaries of this land framing two projects, that I may turn away with my foot to another land, should any one of the watch recognize me while seeking my sister, for they say that she living is united in nuptials and does not remain a virgin, in order that I may converse with her, and, obtaining her for an assistant in the slaughter, may learn clearly the matters within the house. Now therefore, for morn is raising her shining face, we will turn our footsteps out of this track. For either some ploughman or some domestic woman will appear to us, of whom we may inquire whether my sister dwells in this place. But— (for I see some servant coming hither, with shorn hair, bearing a burden of water)—let us sit down, and learn from this female slave, if we can receive any intelligence as to the matters for which, Pylades, we are come to this land.

ELECTRA

Hasten on the course of my foot, O hour; O, go thou on, go on, weeping. Alas! for me, for me. I was born of Agamemnon, and Clyaemnestra, the hateful laughter of Tyndarus, gave me birth, and the citizens call unhappy me Electra. Alas! alas! for my hapless toils and hateful life. O father, but thou indeed art lying in Hades, murdered by thy wife, and by Aegisthus, Agamemnon. Come! raise the same lamentation, lead off the delight of many tears. Haste on the course of my foot, O hour; O go thou on, go on, weeping. Alas! for me, for me. What city, what house, unhappy brother, dost thou serve, leaving thy poor sister in her chambers amid saddest calamities resulting from her sire? O, mayest thou come as a releaser to wretched me from these toils, O Jove, Jove, and as an avenger to thy father of blood most hateful, having neared thy wandering foot to Argos. Let me put down this vessel, taking it off my head, that I may loudly utter gloomy mournings to my sire, a sounding song of Hades, for Hades. O father, to thee beneath the earth I utter lamentations, which ever day by day I ply, gashing my loved neck with my nails, and striking my hand upon my shorn head, on account of thy death. Woe! woe! tear the head, and like some tuneful swan by the river stream calls upon her dearest sire, who has perished in the crafty meshes of a net, so do I mourn thee, my hapless sire, having been washed as to thy flesh with a last bath, in the most piteous bed of death. Alas! for me, for me, for the bitter cutting by an axe, O sire, and the bitter plot on thy return from Troy! Not with mitres nor with garlands did thy wife receive thee; but having made thee the scoff of Aegisthus with the two-edged sword, she obtained her cunning paramour.

CHORUS

Electra, daughter of Agamemnon, I have come to thy rustic home. A certain milk-drinking Mycenian herdsman treading the mountain has come, has come; and he brings word that the Argives are proclaiming the third day of the feast, and all the virgins are about to make procession to Juno.   129

ELECTRA

Not for splendid doings, O friends, nor for golden necklaces, am wretched I elate in mind, nor forming dances together with Argive nymphs shall I beat my foot whirled round. With tears I dance, and tears are the daily care for wretched me. Look at my matted locks, and these rags of my garments, whether they become the royal daughter of Agamemnon, and Troy, which remembers once being taken by my sire.   136

CHORUS

Great is the Goddess; but come, and from me receive richly-woven robes to wear, and golden additions of ornament for thy beauty. Dost thou think, that, not honoring the Gods, thou wilt overcome thine enemies by thy tears? Not with groans, but with prayers, worshipping the Gods, wilt thou obtain a happy day, O daughter.   141

ELECTRA

No one of the Gods hears the voice of (the) wretched, nor the sacrifices offered of old by my sire. Alas! both for the dead, and for the living wanderer, who, I ween, dwells in some other land, wandering wretched to the slaves' hearth, being sprung from a renowned sire. But I myself in a poverty-stricken abode am dwelling, pining away at heart, a fugitive from my ancestral halls, dwelling on the mountain rocks. And my mother dwells wedded in bloody nuptials to another.   148

CHORUS

Helen, thy mother's sister, has the blame of many ills upon the Greeks and thine house.

ELECTRA

Alas! O women, I cease from my lamentations. Some strangers having a station close by the house rise up from their ambush.

Let us escape with flight of foot from the evil-doing men,
you indeed by the road-way, but I into the house.   153

                         ORESTES
     Remain, O wretched one; fear not my hand.

                         ELECTRA
     O Phoebus Apollo! I fall on thy knees that I may not die.

                         ORESTES
     I would fain slay others more hateful than thou.

                         ELECTRA
     Away! touch not what thou shouldst not touch.

                         ORESTES
     There is not one whom I could more rightly touch.   158

                         ELECTRA
     And wherefore, sword in hand, dost thou lay in ambush for
me?

                         ORESTES
     Tarry and listen, and perhaps thou wilt not say otherwise.

                         ELECTRA
     I stand, and am altogether thine, for thou art the more
powerful.

                         ORESTES
     I am come, bearing thee words from thy brother.

                         ELECTRA
     O dearest one, is it of him living or dead?

                         ORESTES
     He lives; I fain would first tell thee the good news.   164

                         ELECTRA
     Mayest thou be blest, as a reward for most pleasant words.

                         ORESTES
     I give this in common for both of us to possess.

                         ELECTRA
     Where on earth is the wretched one enduring a wretched
banishment?

ORESTES
He is wandering, not respecting the law of one city.

ELECTRA
Ay, perhaps in want of daily sustenance.

ORESTES
He possesses it indeed, but is weak as an exiled man.   170

ELECTRA
But what message comest thou bearing from him?

ORESTES
Whether thou art alive, and, living, what fortunes thou
hast.

ELECTRA
Dost thou not first see how dried up is my frame?

ORESTES
Ay, wasted away with grief, so that I utter a groan.

ELECTRA
And my head, and locks savage with being shorn.   175

ORESTES
Thy brother, and thy father's death, I suppose, gnaws thee
equally?

ELECTRA
Alas! for what is dearer to me than these?

ORESTES
Alas! alas! how indeed art thou thought of by thy brother!

ELECTRA
He being absent, not present, is dear to me.

ORESTES
But through what dost thou dwell here, far away from the
city?   180

ELECTRA
I have wedded, O stranger, a deadly wedding.

ORESTES
I grieve for your brother. (Was it) to one of the Mycenians?

ELECTRA

Not in such wise as my father at some time expected to bestow me.

ORESTES

Tell me, that having heard I may tell your brother.

ELECTRA

Far off from him, I dwell in this abode.   185

ORESTES

Some husbandman or neatherd is worthy of such a dwelling.

ELECTRA

A man poor, noble, and pious towards me.

ORESTES

But what piety is present to thine husband?

ELECTRA

He has never ventured to approach my bed.   189

ORESTES

Having some divine feeling of chastity, or disdaining thee?

ELECTRA

He did not think himself worthy to disgrace my parents.

ORESTES

And how was he not delighted on receiving such a match?

ELECTRA

He thinks, O stranger, that he who gave me had no right (to do so).

ORESTES

I understand, lest he should at some time pay the penalty to Orestes.   194

ELECTRA

Fearing this very thing. Besides, he is by nature chaste.

ORESTES

Alas! thou speakest of a noble fellow, and one that must be well treated.

ELECTRA
Ay, if he who now is absent shall ever return to his home.

ORESTES
But did the mother, who bore thee, suffer this?   198

ELECTRA
Women, O stranger, are friends to men, not to children.

ORESTES
But on what account did Aegisthus offer thee this insult?

ELECTRA
He wished me to bring forth a weak race, having given me
to such a man.

ORESTES
That, forsooth, you might not bring forth children as
avengers?   202

ELECTRA
Such things he planned, for which may he pay me the penalty.

ORESTES
But does thy mother's husband know thou art (still) a
virgin?

ELECTRA
He does not know; we have kept this from him in silence.

ORESTES
Are these who overhear our words friends to thee?   206

ELECTRA
Ay, so as to well conceal my words and thine.

ORESTES
What could Orestes do, if he should come to this Argos?

ELECTRA
Dost thou ask this? A foul thing thou sayest, for is it
not now the crisis?

ORESTES
But on his arrival how might he slay the murderers of his
father?   210

ELECTRA
By daring such things as were dared against his father by
his enemies.

ORESTES
And wouldst thou endure to slay thy mother with him?

ELECTRA
Ay, with the same axe by which ray father perished.

ORESTES
Shall I tell these things to him, and is thy resolution
firm?

ELECTRA
Oh might I die, having shed the blood of my mother.   215

ORESTES
Alas! would that Orestes were near to hear this.

ELECTRA
But, stranger, I should not know him, if I saw him.

ORESTES
It is no wonder; for being young, thou wast separated from
him while young.

ELECTRA
One only of my friends would know him.

ORESTES
What, he who they say stole him away from death?   220

ELECTRA
Ay, the old man, the former paedagogue of my father.

ORESTES
And has thy dead father obtained a tomb?

ELECTRA
Cast out of the house, he has obtained what he has obtained.

ORESTES
Alas! What is this thou sayest? For the perception even of
out-door evils pains mortals. But speak, that knowing, I may
bear to thy brother unpleasant words indeed, but needful to
hear. For there is a feeling of pity, not at all in the

untaught, but in the wise of mankind; for it is not even free from harm that a too wise cleverness is in the wise.   229

CHORUS

And I have the same longing at heart as this man. For being far from the city, I know not the ills in the city; but now I also wish to learn.   231

ELECTRA

I will speak, if it behooves me. And it behooves me to tell to a friend the heavy fortunes of me and my father. But since thou hast stirred the subject, I beseech thee, O stranger, to tell Orestes my ills and his. First, indeed, in what garments I live, and with what filth I am weighed down, and under what a roof I dwell, after a royal house; I myself laboring mine own garments with the shuttle, or I should have my body naked and be destitute; and myself bearing the river stream, without a feast at holy rites, and deprived of the dance; and being a virgin, I am denied the rights of women, denied (the bed of) Castor, to whom, being of my family, they affianced me, before he went among the Gods.   242

But my mother sits on a throne, amid Phrygian spoils, and by her seat the Asiatic captives, whom my father took, are standing with their Idaean robes bound with golden clasps. And my father's black blood still putrefies in the house; but he that slew him, mounting the same chariot as my sire, goes forth, and is puffed up, holding in his blood-stained hands the sceptre, with which he ruled the Greeks. But the dishonored tomb of Agamemnon has never received libations nor a bough of myrtle; but the funeral pile is barren of adornments. And the famous spouse (as they call him) of my mother, steeped in drunkenness, leaps on the tomb, and with stones defaces the stone monument of my sire, and dares to utter this saying against us: "Where is the boy Orestes? Will he, being present, honorably defend thy tomb?" Thus is he mocked in his absence. But, O stranger, I beseech thee, tell this news. For many things are they, that lay this charge upon me, but I (am) their interpreter, my hands, my tongue, and wretched mind, and my shorn hair, and his father. For base is it, if my father indeed captured Troy, but he, being one, is unable to slay one man, being a youth, and of a better sire.   262

CHORUS

And truly I perceive this person (I mean your husband) approaching the house, having ceased from labor.

PEASANT

Hah! who are these strangers I see at the gate? And for what reason have they come near this rustic door? Is it in want of myself? surely it is unseemly for a woman to be standing with young men.   266

ELECTRA

O dearest one, do not fall into a suspicion of me. But thou shalt know the real story; for these strangers are come to me as heralds of the words of Orestes. And do ye, O strangers, excuse what has been said.   269

PEASANT

What say they? Is the man alive, and does he behold the light?

ELECTRA

He is, at least by report. And they say things not discredited by me.

PEASANT

Does he at all remember the ills of thy father and of thee?

ELECTRA

These matters are in (my hopes). Weak is an exiled man.

PEASANT

But what words did they come telling from Orestes?

ELECTRA

He has sent these men as spectators of my woes.   275

PEASANT

Some then they see, and others I suppose thou tellest.

ELECTRA

They know (all); they have no deficiency of these.

PEASANT

Long ago then should the doors have been opened to them. Go into the house; for ye shall obtain in return for your good news a hospitable reception in such things as my house contains. Take the baggage within the house, ye followers, and make no denial, having come as friends from a friend. For though I am born poor, I will never show a base-born disposition.   283

ORESTES

By the Gods, is this the man, who joins in concealing your nuptials, not desiring to disgrace Orestes?

ELECTRA

This man is called the husband of wretched me.   285

ORESTES

Alas! there is no certain mark of manliness; for the natures of mortals exhibit a confusion. For already have I seen a man who was naught sprung from a noble sire, and good children (sprung) from bad (fathers), and hunger in the spirit of a rich man, and a great mind in a poor body. How then will any one, distinguishing, judge aright? By wealth? Then he will make use of an unjust judge. Or by those who have nothing? But poverty posesses (this) disease; through want it teaches a man evil. But shall I turn to (the consideration of) arms? But who, looking to the spear, could testify what person is good? It is best to leave these things to take their own course. For this man being neither great among the Argives, nor, on the other hand, puffed up with the reputation of his house, and being among the multitude, has been found most excellent. Will ye not be wise, who wander full of vain opinions? and by association and manners judge of the well born amongst mortals. For such men as these well administer cities and houses; but flesh, destitute of sense, are the ornament of the forum. For neither does the stronger arm better abide the spear than the weak; but this, is in nature and in valor. But,—whether present or not present, the son of Agamemnon, for whose sake we are come, is worthy,—let us accept the hospitality of this house. We must go within this dwelling, servants. For I would rather have a willing, though poor host, than a rich one (unwilling). I therefore accept this man's reception into his house. But I would have wished that your brother prospering could have led me into prospering abodes. But perchance he may come; for the oracles of Loxias are firm, but to the divination of men I bid adieu.   313

CHORUS

Now, more than before, O Electra, we are warmed at heart with joy; for perhaps, though slowly progressing, fortune may (at length) settle well.

ELECTRA

O hapless one, knowing the scantiness of thine house, why hast thou received these strangers superior to thee?   315

PEASANT

But what? If they are, as they seem to be, noble, will they not be equally content with little or not?

ELECTRA

Since then you, being in scant circumstances, have fallen into this mistake, go to the aged guardian of my dear father, who, around the river Tanaus, that divides the confines of the Argive territory and the Spartan land, tends his flocks, having been cast out from the city. And bid him, having come homeward, to go and furnish something as a banquet for the strangers. He will be delighted, and will offer prayers to the Gods, when he hears that the boy is living whom he once saved. For we shall not obtain any thing from my mother out of my ancestral house, and we should be telling bitter news, should the wretched woman learn that Orestes is alive.   327

PEASANT

But, if it seems thus to thee, I will bear this message to the old man. But go thou into the house as quickly as possible, and make ready the matters within. A woman indeed, if willing, can find many things to bring for a banquet. And there is even now so much at home, so as to satisfy these men with food for one clay at least. But when my mind falls upon this subject, I consider how great a power wealth has, both to bestow on strangers, and by expense to preserve one's body when fallen into sickness; but for one's daily food it comes to little. For every man once filled, rich or poor, bears an equality.   337

CHORUS

Ye renowned ships, which once on a time came to Troy with numberless oars, leading the dance with the daughters of Nereus, where the flute-loving dolphin leaped, whirled around the prows with dark blue beaks, escorting the son of Thetis, Achilles, light as to the leaping of his feet, with Agamemnon, to the Trojan shores of Simois. And the daughters of Nereus, quitting the Euboean strand, bore the toils of shield (and) arms (forged) on the golden anvils of Vulcan, both over Pelion, and over the sacred groves of Ossa's height, the nymph-dwelt summits sought the virgins, where the equestrian sire trained up the marine son of Thetis, a light for Greece, Achilles, swift of foot, for the Atridae. And I have heard from some one, who came from Troy to the Nauplian ports, that in the circle of thy renowned shield, son of Thetis, such effigies as these, Phrygian terrors, were sculptured. On the circumference, indeed, of the shield, Perseus, (raised) above the sea with winged slippers, was holding the throat-cut terror of the Gorgon, with Hermes, the messenger of Jove, the rustic son of Maia. But in the midst of the shield the radiant circle of the sun shone with his winged steeds, and the ethereal dances of the stars, the Pleiades, Hyades, terrible to the eyes of Hector. But upon the golden-wrought crest Sphinxes were bearing their song-obtained prey in their claws. And on his cuirass the fiery lioness was hastening in course (after) the Pirenian horse with her hoofs, having beheld it. But in a bloody fight four horses were rushing along, and round their backs the black dust went forth. The king of such spear-laboring men didst thou slay, thy husband, evil-minded daughter of Tyndarus. Wherefore the powers of heaven will send thee down to death, and yet, yet shall I behold the blood poured out by the sword beneath thy gore-streaming neck.

368

OLD MAN

Where, where is my youthful, honored mistress, the daughter of Agamemnon, whom once I nurtured? How steep an approach it is to these dwellings for me, a wrinkled old man, to draw nigh with my foot! But nevertheless I must needs drag on my bent spine and crooked knee. O daughter, (for I but just now behold thee near the house,) I am come bearing to thee this young offspring of my fold, having taken it from the flocks, and garlands,' and cheese which I have taken out of the presses, and this old store of Bacchus, redolent of fragrance, little indeed, but still 'tis sweet to pour a cup of this into a weaker draught. Let some one go and bear these into the house for the strangers. But I, having bedewed mine eyes with tears, would fain wipe them away with this my tattered garment.

381

ELECTRA

But wherefore, O aged man, hast thou thine eye thus wet? Have mine afflictions after a long interval awakened thy remembrance? Or dost thou bemoan the unhappy exile of Orestes, and my sire, whom once holding in thine arras, thou didst in vain nurture for thee and thy friends?

385

OLD MAN

In vain. But nevertheless this at least I could not refrain from. For I came to his tomb, aside from the road, and falling down, I wept, having met with solitude, and I poured out libations, having opened the skin which I bear for the strangers, and set myrtle garlands around the tomb. But upon the pile itself I saw the victim, a sable-fleeced sheep, and the blood but lately shed, and shorn locks of auburn hair. And I marvelled, O daughter, whoever of men had dared to come to the tomb; for it certainly was none of the Argives. But perchance, I think, thy brother has come privily, and on his coming has honored the miserable tomb of his sire. And do thou examine the hair, placing it against thy hair, whether the tint of the shorn tresses is the same. For in those who have the same father's blood, most parts of the body are wont to be naturally alike. 399

ELECTRA

Thou speakest words unworthy of a wise man, O aged one, if thou thinkest that my very bold brother would come by stealth into this land through fear of Aegisthus. Then how will the lock of hair agree, the one belonging to a well-born man brought up in wrestling exercises, but the other to a female (brought up) amidst wool-combing? It is impossible. And thou wilt find similar hair among many persons, though not sprung from the same blood, old man. 406

OLD MAN

But do thou, stepping in his track, consider the print of his slipper, whether it is of the same measure with thy foot, O child. 408

ELECTRA

But how could there be an impression of feet upon the stony surface of the ground? And if it were so, the foot of a brother and sister would not be equal, of a man and woman; but the male prevails. 411

OLD MAN

Is there no (evidence), by which, supposing your brother to have come to the land, you might discern the woof of thy shuttle, in which I once concealed him, lest he should die.

ELECTRA

Knowest thou not, when Orestes was banished from the land, that I was a mere child? But if I did weave the vest, how would he, being then a child, be now wearing the same garments, unless the robes grew along with the body? But either some stranger, pitying his (undecked) tomb, or some one of this land, obtaining (the opportunity of) darkness, has shorn his own hair. 420

OLD MAN
But where are the strangers? for I wish to see, and ask them concerning thy brother.

ELECTRA
Hither with quick step they are coming out from the house.

OLD MAN
And they are noble indeed, but this is superficial; for many born noble, are base; but nevertheless I say to the strangers, hail.

ORESTES
Hail thou! aged man. Of what friend is this man the ancient relict, Electra?   425

ELECTRA
He nurtured my sire, stranger.

ORESTES
What sayest thou? Was this hu who privily removed thy brother?

ELECTRA
This is he who saved him, it he indeed is yet in being.

ORESTES
Ah! why has he gazed on me, as though viewing the clear stamp of silver? Does he liken me to any one?

ELECTRA
Perchance he is pleased at looking on thee, a compeer of Orestes.   430

ORESTES
Ay, of a well-loved man; but wherefore does he turn his step around me?

ELECTRA
I too marvel as I behold this, O stranger.

OLD MAN
O revered daughter Electra, adore the deities.

ELECTRA
In respect of what things absent or present?   434

OLD MAN
For holding the cherished treasure, which a God shows thee.

ELECTRA
Lo! I call upon the Gods. Or what dost thou mean indeed,
old man?

OLD MAN
Look then upon this most beloved one, O child.

ELECTRA
Long since I fear lest thou art no longer in thy right
senses.

OLD MAN
Am I not in my right senses, beholding thy brother?

ELECTRA
How sayest thou this incredible saying, O aged man?   440

OLD MAN
That in this man I see Orestes, the son of Agamemnon.

ELECTRA
Perceiving what indication, by which I may be persuaded?

OLD MAN
A scar near upon his forehead, by which once in his father's
house he, falling, was stained with blood, pursuing with thee
a hind.   444

ELECTRA
How sayest thou? I see indeed the evidence of the fall.

OLD MAN
And then dost thou delay to fall upon those most dear?

ELECTRA
But no longer so, O aged man; for in mind I am persuaded
by thy proofs. O thou who appearest after a long season,
unexpectedly I hold thee.

ORESTES
Ay, and by me thou art held after a long season.

ELECTRA
Never did I expect it.   450

ORESTES

Nor did I hope it.

ELECTRA

Art thou he?

ORESTES

Ay, thine only ally, if indeed I can but draw up (successfully) the net after which I am going. But I have a good trust; or it behooves one no longer to think that there are Gods, if unjust deeds get the advantage of justice.   456

CHORUS

Thou hast come, thou hast come, day, after a long time; thou hast shone out, thou hast shown forth a clear torch to the city, which wretched during a long exile from an ancestral home has come wandering. Some God, some God again brings on our victory. Uplift your hands, uplift your voice, send forth prayers to the Gods, that thy brother may enter the city with good fortune, with good fortune.   462

ORESTES

Be it so. I indeed have the sweet pleasure of embraces, but in time again we shall bestow them. But do thou say, aged man, (for thou hast come in season,) by what doing shall I punish the murderer of my father, and my mother, partaker of an unholy marriage. Is there aught of friends well-disposed towards me? Or have I prepared all things, according to fortunes? With whom shall I confederate? By night, or by day? By what road shall I turn against mine enemies?   469

OLD MAN

O son, to thee unhappy no one is a friend. For this thing is (indeed) a discovery, to share good and evil in common. But do thou (for thou art utterly undone from the very foundations, in respect to thy friends, nor hast thou left any hope) know this, hearing from me. In thy hand and fortune thou hast all the chance of recovering thy ancestral house and city.   475

ORESTES

By doing then what, shall we reach this end?

OLD MAN

By slaying the son of Thyestes and thy mother.

ORESTES

I am come for this crown (of success), and how shall I obtain it?

OLD MAN

Not by going indeed within the walls, even if you wished.

ORESTES

Is he protected by the guards and their right hands?   480

OLD MAN

Thou hast hit it; for he fears you, and sleeps not in certainty.

ORESTES

Well! do thou then henceforward advise, old man.

OLD MAN

And do thou hear me; for something has just come into my thoughts.

ORESTES

Mayest thou give some good advice, and I hear it.

OLD MAN

I saw Aegisthus as I was coming slowly hither—   485

ORESTES

I attend to what you have said. In what place?

OLD MAN

Near upon these horse-pasturing meadows.

ORESTES

Doing what? For I see help out of things inextricable.

OLD MAN

He was preparing a banquet for the Nymphs, as it seemed to me.

ORESTES

As a payment for his son's nurturing, or for future offspring?   490

OLD MAN

I know but one thing; he had armed himself for the slaughter of a bull.

ORESTES
With how many companions? Or was he alone with his domestics?

OLD MAN
No Argive was present, but his own band (of servants).

ORESTES
Is there any one who will know me, when he sees me, old man?   494

OLD MAN
His servants only are present, who have never seen thee.

ORESTES
But would they be friendly to us, if we prevailed?

OLD MAN
Ay, for this is peculiar to slaves, and useful to thee.

ORESTES
How, then, should I even approach him?

OLD MAN
Going (to a place) where he will see thee, as he is sacrificing.

ORESTES
He is in the fields by the way itself, as it seems.   500

OLD MAN
Ay, from whence espying thee, he will invite you to share his banquet.

ORESTES
In truth a bitter fellow-banqueter, if God be willing.

OLD MAN
Observe henceforward according to the occasion.

ORESTES
Well hast thou spoken. But where is my mother?   504

OLD MAN
At Argos; but she will come to the drinking and banquet.

ORESTES

But wherefore did not my mother set out at once with her
husband?

OLD MAN

She was left, dreading the reproach of the citizens.

ORESTES

I understand. She knows that she is suspected by the city.

OLD MAN

So it is; for an impious woman is hated.   509

ORESTES

How then shall I slay at once both her and this fellow?

ELECTRA

I indeed will contrive the death of my mother.

ORESTES

And truly fortune shall set that matter right.

ELECTRA

Let then this man help us, being two.

OLD MAN

This shall be. But how wilt thou devise death for thy
mother?

ELECTRA

(Go and say thus, old man, to Clyaemnestra.) Bear word that
I am brought to bed in labor of a male.   515

OLD MAN

Whether having brought forth some time since, or lately?

ELECTRA

Ten suns; during which the woman in labor is purified.

OLD MAN

But what in truth does this tend to thy mother's death?

ELECTRA

She will come, when she has heard of my childbirth
sickness.

OLD MAN
Whence? What dost thou think she cares, child?   520

ELECTRA
Yea, and she will bemoan the dignity of my offspring.

OLD MAN
Perhaps so; I lead thy discourse back to the point of turning.

ELECTRA
It is plain that she will perish when she has come.

OLD MAN
And truly let her come to the very gates of the dwelling.

ELECTRA
Is it not a little thing to turn to Hades?   525

OLD MAN
Would that I might die, having sometime beheld this.

ELECTRA
Then first of all lead the way for this person, old man.

OLD MAN
(What to) where Aegisthus is now sacrificing to the Gods?

ELECTRA
Then meeting my mother, deliver my message.   529

OLD MAN
Ay, so that it shall seem to be spoken by thy own mouth.

ELECTRA
'Tis thy task now. Thou art allotted first to begin the slaughter.

ORESTES
I will go, if any one will be leader of the way.

OLD MAN
And in truth I will escort thee not unwillingly.

ORESTES
O thou ancestral Jove, putter to flight of mine enemies, pity us, for we have suffered pitiable things.

ELECTRA

Ay, pity those who are born thy descendants.   535

ORESTES

And thou, Juno, who rulest over the Mycenian altars, grant us the victory, if we crave just things.

ELECTRA

Give indeed to us an avenging power for our sire.

ORESTES

And thou who impiously dost dwell below the earth, father, (and thou queen Earth, to whom I stretch forth my hands,) aid, aid these thy dearest children. Now come. taking all the dead as allies, as many as with thee destroyed the Phrygians with the spear, and as many as hate impious assassins. Hast thou heard, O thou that hast suffered dreadful things from my mother?   543

ELECTRA

Father hears all, I know; but it is time to go. And to thee I proclaim moreover that Aegisthus must die. So that, if in contest thou shalt fall a deadly fall, I also am dead; nor speak of me as living; for I will smite my head with a two-edged sword. But going within the dwelling, I will make ready, so that, should prosperous tidings of thee arrive, the whole house shall shout aloud; but if thou diest, the contrary of these things will be. I tell thee this.   550

ORESTES

I know all.

ELECTRA

Therefore it behooves thee to be a man. But do you, O women, well light up the shout of this contest. But I will keep guard, carrying in my hand a ready spear. For never, overcome by my enemies, will I pay the penalty for my body to be abused.   555

CHORUS

A report remains in the ancient traditions of the Argive mountains, that once on a time Pan, the guardian of the fields, breathing forth a sweet-sounding song on the well-compacted reeds, conducted from its tender mother a ram with beauteous fleece of gold. And standing on a rocky-bench, a herald exclaimed, "To the forum, to the forum come, O Mycenians, about to behold prodigies, (and) fearful visions of happy rulers." And choirs of the sons of Atreus adorned the dwelling, and the gold-decked temples were opened, and on the altars through the city the fire offered by the Argives blazed. And the pipe, the minister of the Muses, sent forth a most beauteous sound, and delightful songs increased concerning the golden lamb, as praises of Thyestes. 567

For having seduced the dear wife of Atreus to clandestine nuptials, he bears off the prodigy to his home, and returning to the assembly, he proclaims that he possessed the golden-fleeced horned flock in his dwelling. Then indeed, then Jove changed the shining paths of the stars, and the light of the Sun, and the white face of Morn, and to the western side he drives (them) with warm flames glittering from heaven, and the damp clouds (go) towards the north, and the dry seats of Hammon are parched for lack of moisture, deprived of the fairest showers from Jove. It is said (but with me, at least, it has little credit) that the golden-visaged sun turned away, having changed his warm station through a mortal misfortune, on account of mortal justice. But stories terrible to mortals are a gain for the worship of the Gods; of which thou being unmindful, hast slain thy husband, thou joint mother of noble children." Hold, hold, my friends, heard ye a noise? or has a vain opinion possessed me, like as the nether thundering of Jove? Behold! these sounds are wafted not indistinct. My mistress Electra, pass out of this dwelling. 585

ELECTRA
My friends, what is the matter? To what peril are we come?

CHORUS
I know but one thing, I hear a shriek of death.

ELECTRA
I also heard it, far off indeed, but yet (I heard it).

CHORUS
Ay, for sound comes a long distance, and still clear.

ELECTRA
Is it the groan of an Argive, or of my friends? 590

CHORUS
I know not; for all the tone of the cry is confused.

ELECTRA
Thou enjoinest this as a death to me; why do we hesitate?

CHORUS
Stop! that thou mayest clearly learn thy fortunes.

ELECTRA
It cannot be. We are vanquished; for where are the messengers?

CHORUS
They will come; it is no easy task to kill a king.   595

MESSENGER
O ye victorious Mycenian virgins, I pronounce to all his friends that Orestes is victorious, and that the murderer of Agamemnon, Aegisthus, lies on the ground; and it is meet to adore the Gods.

ELECTRA
And who art thou? How dost thou signify to me things certain?

MESSENGER
Knowest thou not that thou beholdest in me an attendant on thy brother.   600

ELECTRA
O dearest one, through fear indeed I had a difficulty in recognizing thy face; but now indeed I know thee. What sayest thou? Is my father's hated murderer dead?

MESSENGER
He is dead; I tell thee twice, what thou indeed wishest.

CHORUS
O Gods, and Justice, that beholdest all things, thou hast come at last.

ELECTRA
But in what manner and by what system of slaughter he slew the son of Thyestes I desire to learn.   605

MESSENGER
After we had withdrawn our footsteps from these dwellings, we entered upon a dividing wagon-road, where was the renowned king of the Mycenians. And he chanced to be walking in his well-watered gardens, cropping for his head branches of tender myrtle. And on seeing us, he cries out: O strangers, who are ye? Whence come ye, and of what land are ye? And

Orestes replied: "We are Thessalians, and are come to Alpheus in order to sacrifice to Olympian Jove." And Aegisthus, hearing this, speaks thus: "Now indeed ye must be as my hearth-sharers in the feast; for I happen to be sacrificing a bull to the Nymphs; but having risen in the morning from bed ye will go the same way. But let us go within the house." And, thus saying, he took us by the hand, and led us on; nor was it right to refuse. But when we were within the house, he speaks thus: "Let some one with all speed bring lavers for the guests, that they may stand round the altar near the lustral vessels." But Orestes answered: "We are but lately purified in pure baths from river streams. But if it befit strangers to join with the citizens in sacrifice we are ready, king Aegisthus, and refuse not.". This conference then they both broke off in the middle; and the servants, having laid down the spears, the protection of their master, all set their hands to work. Some bore a vessel to catch the blood; others uplifted the canisters; others kindled the fire, and placed the cauldrons round the hearth; and the whole roof echoed.

But the partner of thy mother's bed, taking the salted cakes, cast them on the altar, speaking such words as these: "Ye Nymphs of the rock, (grant) that I may often sacrifice a bull, as also my wife within the house, the daughter of Tyndarus, faring as we do now; but that my enemies (may fare) ill"—meaning Orestes and thee. But my master prayed the opposite—not speaking aloud—that he might recover his ancestral home. And Aegisthus, taking a straight knife out of the canister, cut off (some of) the bullock's hair, and placed it on the pure flame with his right hand; then he slew the bullock on the shoulders of the servants, as they lifted it with their hands, and speaks thus to thy brother: "They boast that this is among the noble deeds of the Thessalians, to dissect a bull skillfully, and to rein in horses. Take the steel, stranger, and prove that the report concerning the Thessalians is true." But he, having seized in his hands the well-wrought Doric blade, stripping off the well-fastened robe from his shoulders, took Pylades, indeed, as an assistant in the toil, and pushed away the domestics.   648

Then seizing the foot of the bullock, he laid bare the white flesh, stretching out his hand, and more quickly stripped off the skin than a horse courser could finish twice twelve hundred paces, and he opened the flank. And Aegisthus, taking the entrails in his hands, examined them. But the lobe was not in the entrails; and the entrance (of the liver) and the receptacle the bile denoted evil attacks upon the searcher. And he indeed knit his brow; but my master asked, "Wherefore art thou sad, stranger?" (He replied): "I fear some foreign plot; for the son of Agamemnon is most detested, and is hostile to mine house." But he replied: "Dost thou dread the stratagem of a wanderer, being ruler over the city? Will not some one exchange for us a Phthian chopper instead of a Dorian, that we may celebrate the banquet of inspection? I will cleave open the breast." Then holding, he cleaves it; and Aegisthus, taking the entrails, contemplated them, having separated them. But as he stooped down, thy brother, standing on tip-toe, smote him on the spine, and broke the joints of his back. And all his body was convulsed up and down, and he howled, dying with difficulty from the death-blow. But when the servants beheld it, they forthwith rushed to arms, being many to fight against two; but through their valor Pylades and Orestes stood brandishing their weapons before their faces. And he (Orestes) said: "I am not come as an enemy to this city, nor to my subjects, but I, the hapless Orestes, have avenged myself on the murderer of my sire. Slay me not then, ye ancient domestics of my sire." But they, after they heard his words, restrained their spears; and he was recognized by some aged veteran in the house. And straightway they crown the head of thy brother, rejoicing, shouting. And he comes to thee to show the head, not bearing that of the Gorgon, but of him thou hatest, Aegisthus. But blood for blood has come upon him, who now dies, as the bitter payment for a debt.   681

CHORUS

Place thy step for a dance, dear one, like a fawn, with delight lightly moving its bounding aloft. Thy brother conquers, having accomplished a garland-bearing better than by the streams of Alpheus. But chant a strain of victory for my dance.   685

ELECTRA

O light, O splendor of the four-horsed sun, O earth, and night, which I before beheld, now mine eye, and ye folds (of heaven) now free, since Aegisthus, my father's murderer, has fallen. Come, I must bring out whatever ornaments for the hair I (possess) and my dwellings conceal, O friends, and I will crown the head of my victorious brother.   691

CHORUS

Do you then bring forth ornaments for the head; but on our part the dance loved by the Muses shall proceed. Now our former well-beloved kings rule our land, having justly put down the unjust; and let a shout go forth, attuned to joy.

ELECTRA

O thou with a glorious victory, born of a sire victorious in the war under Troy, Orestes, receive fillets for the locks of thine hair. For thou art come to thy home, not as having run an useless contest of six plethra, but having slain the enemy Aegisthus, who destroyed thine and my sire. And do thou, Pylades, a shield companion, (and) nursling of a most pious man, receive a garland from my hand; for thou too bearest an equal share of the contest with this man; and may ye ever appear to me fortunate.

702

ORESTES

Think in the first place, Electra, that the Gods are the leaders of this fortune, and then commend me, the minister of the Gods and of fortune. For I am come, having slain Aegisthus not in word, but in deed; and to give any one the power of knowing this clearly, I bring the dead himself to thee; whom, if thou wilt, expose as a prey to wild beasts, or, fixing to a stake, stick him down, a booty for birds, the children of the sky. For he is now thy slave, having before been called thy master.

710

ELECTRA

I am ashamed, yet wish to speak.

ORESTES

What is it, speak; since thou art far off from fear.

ELECTRA

(I fear) to insult the dead, lest some one smite me with invidiousness.

ORESTES

There is no one who could blame thee.

ELECTRA

Our city is hard to please, and fond of slander.

715

ORESTES

Speak, if thou desirest, sister; for we have entered upon enmity with this person upon terms that admit of no treaty.

ELECTRA

(To the corpse of AEGISTHUS.)

Well then, what beginning of reproaches shall I address to thee? What end? what middle discourse shall I draw out? And truly from the dawn I never ceased muttering what I wished to say to thy face, had I indeed been free from my former fears. Now then I am so; and I will repay thee those words of ill which I would have said to thee living. Thou didst destroy me, and, naught injured, didst make me and this man bereft of a dear father, and didst shamefully marry my mother, and murder her husband, the leader of the Grecian army, not having (thyself) gone against the Phrygians. And to such an extent of folly didst thou come, that thou didst hope to find my mother not wicked towards thee, but thou didst injure my father's bed. But let a man know, when after having corrupted a man's wile with secret nuptials, he is subsequently compelled to take her, that he is a wretched being, if he thinks that she in the one case will be unmindful of chastity, but will be mindful of it with him. And most miserably didst thou live, not thinking to live ill; for thou knewest indeed that thou hadst made an unholy marriage, and my mother (knew) that she in thee possessed an impious husband. But being an evil pair, ye obtained your fortune, she thine evil one, and thou hers. And among all the Argives thou didst hear such words as these: "See that woman's slave," not "the husband's wife." But surely this is base, for the woman, not the man, to rule the household; and I loathe those children, who are named in the city not from the male sire, but from the mother. For when a man marries a conspicuous and superior match, of the man there is no account, but of the woman. Which thing has most deceived thee, not knowing it. Thou didst boast to be somebody, relying on thy wealth; but wealth is naught, except to tarry with us for a little time.   746

But nature is stable; not money: since the one ever remaining uplifts her head; but wealth unjust, and dwelling with the foolish, is wont to flit from the house, having flourished for a short season. But for the matters regarding women I am silent; for it is not seemly fur a virgin to speak (of them), and knowingly I will but hint. Thou didst wanton, as possessing, forsooth, a regal palace, and as being firm in beauty. But may my husband be he, who has not the face of a virgin, but of manly manner. For their children depend on Mars; but mere prettiness is an ornament only in the dance. Perdition seize thee, ignorant of all; for which, in time detected, thou hast paid the penalty, being thus an evil-doer. Let not a man, if he run the first course well, think he will win the victory, before he comes nigh the line, and turns the end of life.   760

CHORUS

He has done dreadful deeds, and a dreadful retribution has he paid to thee and this man. For a mighty strength does justice possess.

ORESTES

Be it so. It behooves you, servants, to bear the body of this man within, and to give it to darkness, that when my mother comes, she may not see the corse before (her own) death.

764

ELECTRA

Stop! Let us throw ourselves upon another topic.

ORESTES

What? dost thou see auxiliary troops from Mycenae?

ELECTRA

No, but the mother, who gave me birth.

ORESTES

Opportunely indeed, she comes into the midst of the snare.

ELECTRA

And truly she is brilliant in her chariot and robes.

ORESTES

What then shall we do? shall we murder our mother?

770

ELECTRA

Does pity possess thee, as soon as thou seest thy mother's person?

ORESTES

Alas! for how shall I slay her, who bore and nourished me?

ELECTRA

Like as she destroyed thy sire and mine.

ORESTES

O Phoebus, much folly indeed hast thou prophesied—

ELECTRA

But where Apollo is foolish, who are wise?

775

ORESTES
Who hast bidden me to slay my mother, whom it is not
fitting.

ELECTRA
But in what art thou harmed, avenging thy father?

ORESTES
Having been then pure, I shall now be accused of my mother's
murder.

ELECTRA
Ay, and not avenging thy father, thou wilt be impious.

ORESTES
But I shall pay to my mother the penalty of death.   780

ELECTRA
But to whom, on the other hand, shouldst thou abandon the
avenging of thy sire?

ORESTES
Did not some demon, likened to the God, enjoin that?

ELECTRA
What, sitting on the sacred tripod? I opine not.

ORESTES
I cannot be persuaded that this was a genuine response.

ELECTRA
Thou shalt not through cowardice fall into unmanliness.

ORESTES
Shall I then contrive the same artifice against her?

ELECTRA
Ay, by which thou also didst destroy her husband Aegisthus,
having slain him.   787

ORESTES
I will enter in; but I am beginning a dreadful attempt.
Ay, and I shall do dreadful things; but if this seems fit to
the Gods, let it be; but the contest is for me (at once)
bitter and sweet.   790

CHORUS

Ho! thou royal lady of the land of Argos, daughter of Tyndarus, and sister of the twin noble sons of Jove, who inhabit the flaming ether, amid the stars, having honors from mortals as protectors amidst the waves of the sea. Hail! I reverence you equally with the Gods, because of your wealth and great happiness. And it is now the season for thy fortunes, O queen, to be respected by all.   796

CLYTEMNESTRA

Descend from the chariot, ye Trojan damsels, and lay hold of my hand, that I may place my foot outside this car. For the houses indeed of the Gods are adorned with Phrygian spoils; but I possess in my house these, chosen from the Trojan land, in place of the daughter whom I lost, a small but honorable gift.   801

ELECTRA

Shall I not then, mother, (for I am a slave cast out of my ancestral home and inhabit an unhappy dwelling,) take hold of thy happy hand?

CLYTEMNESTRA

These slaves are present. Do not thou labor for me?

ELECTRA

What, hast thou not dislodged me, in truth, as a slave from the house? for when mine house was taken, I was taken, like as these women, being left destitute of a father.   806

CLYTEMNESTRA

Such plans indeed did thy sire devise against those friends against whom it least behooved him. But I will speak, although, when a wrong opinion possesses a woman, there is a certain bitterness upon her tongue, (as indeed is the case with us,) not fitly indeed; but it is just that we hate, when we have learnt the matter, if indeed one has right grounds for hating. But if not, why should one hate? Now Tyndarus bestowed me on thy sire, not that I nor my children should perish. But that man, having persuaded my daughter by the (pretended) nuptials of Achilles, went from home leading her from the ship-receiving Aulis, where stretching her above the pile, he cut through the fair cheek of Iphigenia. Now if, to prevent the capture of a city, or to benefit his house, and save his other children, he had slain one on behalf of many, it would have been pardonable; but now because Helen was a wanton, and he who had recovered her knew not how to chastise a traitorous wife, on this account he (Agamemnon) destroyed my child. At this, then, although injured, I was not rendered savage, nor would I have slain my husband. But he came to me bringing a raving God-possessed girl, and introduced her to his bed, and would have had two wives at once in the same dwelling. Now women are foolish, I will not deny it; but when this being the case, a husband errs, by neglecting the bed in his home, a wife is wont to imitate her husband, and possess another love. And then the blame shines forth upon us; but the men, who are the cause of this, are in no bad repute. But if Menelaus had been privily carried off from home, must I needs have slain Orestes, that I might preserve Menelaus my sister's husband? And how would thy sire have tolerated this? Was it then right that he indeed should not die, having slain my (children), but that I should suffer at his hands? I slew him; I turned myself the way that lay open to his enemies. For who of your father's friends would have shared the deed with me? Say, if thou desirest aught, and lay down with freedom, on the other side, that thy father died not justly.

ELECTRA

Thou hast spoken justly; but even justice has something of disgrace; for it behooves a woman who is in her senses to yield to her husband in all things. But if this seems not so, neither does it come into the account of my words. Remember, mother, the last words thou didst say, in permitting me to speak to thee with freedom. 846

CLYTEMNESTRA

Ay, and I say so now, and deny not, child.

ELECTRA

But wilt thou, O mother, treat me ill, when thou hast heard? 848

CLYTEMNESTRA

Not so; but I will add what is pleasant to thy feelings.

ELECTRA

I will speak then: and this is the beginning of my prelude. Would that, O mother, thou hadst possessed a wiser mind. For the form indeed both of Helen and thee is worthy to bear commendation; but ye were born twin sisters, both wanton, and not worthy of Castor. For she indeed being carried off, willingly was lost; but thou hast destroyed the best man of Greece, alleging a pretence, that thou didst slay thy husband on thy child's account (for they know not well the facts, as

I do); thou who, before the sacrifice of thy daughter was completed, and when thy husband had but lately set out from home, didst adorn the auburn tresses of thine hair before a mirror. But a woman who, while her husband is absent from home, decks herself out for beauty, writes herself down as evil. For it behooves her to show not at all her fair face out of doors, unless she is seeking some wickedness. But I know that thou alone of all the Grecian women didst rejoice, if the Trojan affairs prospered; but, if they had the worst, that thou didst wear a clouded look, not wishing Agamemnon to return from Troy. And yet there were good reasons for thee to be chaste. 868

Thou hadst a husband not worse than Aegisthus, whom Greece chose for her general; and when thy sister Helen had done such deeds, it was in thy power to obtain great renown; for evil deeds furnish an example and contemplation to the good. But if, as thou sayest, my father slew thy daughter, how have I and my brother injured thee? Why then didst thou not, having slain thy husband, unite to us ancestral houses? but thou carried off stranger nuptials, purchasing a husband for hire. And neither is thy husband (Aegisthus) banished on account of thy son (Orestes), nor is he dead on my account, twice having slain me on account of my sister (Iphigenia)? 878

But if slaughter shall requite slaughter, I and thy son Orestes must slay thee, avenging our father. For if those deeds were just, these are just likewise. But whosoever, looking to wealth or nobility, marries a wicked woman, is a fool; for an humble, yet modest partner is better in one's house, than a powerful one. 883

CHORUS

There is a fatality in the nuptials of women; for I perceive that among mortals some marriages fall out well, some not well. 885

CLYTEMNESTRA

O daughter, thou wert born to love ever thy sire. And this is the case: some side with the males; but others love their mother rather than their father. I will pardon thee; for in truth, my child, I do not so very much rejoice in what I have done. But thus unwashed, and with thy form thus badly clothed, hast thou just ceased from thy throes in child-birth? Alas I wretched me for my devices; how have I stirred my husband to wrath more than was fitting! 892

ELECTRA

Thou mournest late, when thou hast no remedy. My father is dead; but why dost thou not recall thy son who is wandering out of this land?

CLYTEMNESTRA

I have a fear, and consider my own interests, not his. For he is angered, as they say, at the death of his father.   895

ELECTRA

Why then dost thou keep thy husband furious against us?

CLYTEMNESTRA

Such are his manners; and thou also art self-willed.

ELECTRA

For I am pained; but I will cease being self-willed.

CLYTEMNESTRA

And truly he shall no longer be harsh to thee.

ELECTRA

He is very proud, for he dwells in my house.   900

CLYTEMNESTRA

Dost thou see? Thou art again fanning new quarrels.

ELECTRA

I will be silent, for I fear him, as I fear him.

CLYTEMNESTRA

Cease from these words. But wherefore didst thou call me, child?

ELECTRA

Thou hast heard, I suppose, of my being brought to bed. On this account do thou offer sacrifice for me, (for I know not how,) on the tenth day of the month from the child's birth,' as is the custom. For I am not experienced, being hitherto childless.   907

CLYTEMNESTRA

This is the task of another, who has acted as midwife.

ELECTRA

I myself was my midwife, and alone brought forth an infant.

CLYTEMNESTRA
Dost thou inhabit a home so neighborless of friends?   910

ELECTRA
No one desires to possess the poor as friends.

CLYTEMNESTRA
But I will go, that I may sacrifice for the accomplished number of the child's (days); but after I have done this favor for thee, I will go to the field where my husband is offering sacrifices to the Nymphs. But ye, attendants, leading these harnessed steeds, place them in the stalls; but when ye think that I am released from this sacrifice to the Gods, be at hand; for it behooves me also to do favor to my husband.   917

ELECTRA
Enter into our poor abode; but take care lest the smoky roof discolor thy robes, for thou shalt make such a sacrifice to the Gods as behooves thee.
(CLYTEMNESTRA goes in.)
For the canister is ready, and the knife whetted, which has already destroyed the bull, near whom thou stricken shalt fall. And even in the house of Hades thou shalt be united to him with whom thou didst sleep during life. So great a favor will I bestow on thee; and thou on me an atonement for my father.   924

CHORUS
A requital for evils, changed gales for the house are blowing. Then indeed in the bath my lord, my lord fell, and the house shrieked, and the stone-pinnacles of the house, as he spake thus: "O wretched woman, why dost thou slay me returning to my dear country after ten corn-seasons?" But a changing tide of justice secretly leads on this woman, wretched on account of her changed bed; who having taken an axe in her hands, slew with the sharp-whetted blade by her own hand her wretched husband, returning after a long season to his house and the Cyclopeian sky-capping walls. A wretched husband, in that he had a wretched woman for a bane! Like as a mountain lioness, pasturing amidst the oak-thickets of the woods, she wrought these deeds.   936

CLYTEMNESTRA
O children, by the Gods, slay not your mother.

CHORUS
Dost thou hear the noise beneath the roof?

CLYTEMNESTRA

Alas! for me, for me!

CHORUS

I also bewail her murdered by her children. In truth the deity regulates justice, when there is a chance. Wretchedly hast thou suffered; but impious deeds hast thou done to thy husband, unhappy one. But hither these direct their foot from the house, defiled with the new-shed blood of their mother, terrible evidences of her hapless addresses (to them). There is not, nor ever was a house more wretched than that of the descendants of Tantalus.   946

ORESTES

O earth and Jove, that surveyest all mortal things, behold these bloody, horrid deeds, two bodies prostrate on the ground, by a blow from my hand, a requital of mine ills.

ELECTRA

Mournful matters indeed, O brother, but I am the cause. Through lire 1 have wretched gone against this my mother, who gave me, her daughter, birth. Alas! for thy fortune, thy fortune, mother that didst give me birth; thou that hast suffered accursed things, wretched and more than (wretched), at the hands of thy children. But justly hast thou atoned for my father's murder.   954

ORESTES

Alas! Phoebus, thou didst enjoin justice; thou hast wrought publicly griefs not to be told, and hast given bloody nuptials from Greece. But to what other city can I go? What host, what pious friend will look upon the face of me a matricide?

ELECTRA

Alas! alas for me! And whither shall I? to what dance, to what nuptials, shall I go? What husband will receive me to a bridal bed?   960

ORESTES

Again, again has thy disposition changed (with the gale); for thou now hast pious thoughts, not having them then; but thou, O dear one, hast done dreadful things towards thy unwilling brother. Didst thou see how the wretched woman threw aside her robes, and showed her bosom during the slaughter, alas! for me, bending her knees to the earth? But I was like to faint.   966

ELECTRA

I well know thou wast in grief, hearing the piteous groan of the mother who bore thee.

ORESTES

And she uttered such a cry as this, placing her hand on my beard, "My child, I beseech thee;" and she hung upon my cheeks, so that the sword fell from my hands.   969

CHORUS

Oh! wretched one, how hast thou had the heart to behold in thy sight the slaughter of thy mother breathing her last?

ORESTES

I indeed casting my robes upon mine eyes, began (the slaughter) with my sword, driving it into my mother's neck.

ELECTRA

And I indeed encouraged thee; and at the same time laid hands on the sword. You have done the most dreadful of deeds.

ORESTES

Take hold, take hold, cover the limbs of my mother with garments, close up her wounds. Murderers in truth didst thou give birth to for thyself.   975

ELECTRA

See, thee a friend, yet not a friend, we cover with garments, a finish of the great ills in the house.

CHORUS

But hither above the summit of the house appear some demons, or of the heavenly Gods; for this is no path for mortals. Why come they into the clear sight of mortals?   979

CASTOR and POLLUX
(Appearing.)

O son of Agamemnon, listen; for the twin brothers of thy mother, the sons of Jove, call upon thee, Castor, and this his brother Pollux. But having lately appeased a terrible storm of the ocean, we have come to Argos, when we saw the slaughter of this our sister, thy mother. She then has what was just, but thou dost not so; and Phoebus, Phoebus—but 1 will be silent, for he is my king—but being wise, he prophesied to thee things not wise. But we must needs acquiesce in this. But henceforth it behooves thee to perform what Fate and Jove have decreed concerning thee. On Pylades, indeed, bestow Electra as a wife for his house; but do thou leave Argos, for it is not for thee to tread this land, having slain thy mother. But the dreadful Furies, the dog-visaged Goddesses, will drive thee maddened to roam astray. And when thou shalt arrive at Athens, embrace the hallowed image of Minerva; for she will drive them off, terrified by her terrible dragons, so as not to touch thee, stretching forth the Gorgon-faced circle over thine head. Now there is a certain hill of Mars, where the Gods first sate in vote concerning blood, when savage Mars, in wrath for the impious nuptials of his daughter, slew Halirrothius, the son of the ruler of the ocean, where from that (time) there is a most pious and firm judgment for the Gods. Here it behooves thee also to run the gauntlet concerning murder. But votes being placed equal will preserve thee from dying by justice; for Loxias will take the blame upon himself, having commanded the murder of your mother. 1005

And to those hereafter this law shall be fixed, that the defendant shall always escape by equal votes. The fearful Goddesses indeed, stricken with this vexation, will sink into a chasm of the earth near the hill itself, a sacred pious oracle (hereafter) for mortals. But thee it behooves to dwell in a city on the streams of Alpheus, near the Lycaean enclosure; and the city shall be called after thy name. To thee indeed I have thus spoken; but this corse of Aegisthus the citizens of Argos shall conceal in a tomb of earth. But Menelaus, who has just arrived at Nauplia, since he has conquered the Trojan land, and Helen, will bury thy mother. For (Helen) is come from the house of Proteus, having left Egypt; nor did she go to the Phrygians. But Jove, in order that strife and slaughter of mortals might arise, sent an image of Helen to Troy. Let Pylades then, having this damsel as his wife, return to his home in the Achaian land, and bear him who is nominally thy brother-in-law into the land of the Phocians, and give him weight of wealth. But do thou, passing with thy foot over the neck of the Isthmian land, go towards the prosperous house of Cecropia; for having fulfilled thy destined fate (resulting) from this murder, thou wilt be happy, being freed from these ills. 1026

CHORUS

O sons of Jove, is it lawful for us to approach thy converse?

CASTOR and POLLUX

It is lawful, for those not polluted by these murders.

ORESTES
And may I share in speech, sons of Tyndarus?   1029

CASTOR and POLLUX
Thou mayest. I will lay this deed of blood upon Phoebus.

CHORUS
How, being Gods and brothers of this woman who hast perished, did ye not avert the calamities from these houses?

CASTOR and POLLUX
Destiny of necessity led on her fate, and the unwise words of the tongue of Phoebus.

ELECTRA
But what Apollo (compelled) me? What oracles pronounced that I should be the murderess of my mother?

CASTOR and POLLUX
Common was the deed, and common the fate; and one curse of your sires has harassed both.

ORESTES
O sister mine, seeing thee after a long time, I am immediately deprived of thine endearments, and, left by thee, I leave thee.   1035

CASTOR and POLLUX
She has a husband and home. She has not suffered things to be pitied, save that she leaves her Argive city.

ORESTES
And what other greater cause is there for groaning, than to leave the boundaries of one's country? But I shall go out from my father's house, and undergo the charge of murder of my mother at the votes of others.   1039

CASTOR and POLLUX
Be of good cheer. Thou wilt come to the holy city of Pallas. But bear up.

ELECTRA
Join thy breast to my breast, O dearest brother; for the bloody curses of our mother disjoin us from our ancestral home.

ORESTES

Throw thy body closely, hug me; and weep, as on the tomb
of me dead.   1044

CASTOR and POLLUX

Alas! alas! thou hast uttered this a terrible thing even
for Gods to hear. For in me and in the inhabitants of heaven
there is pity fur much-toiling mortals.

ORESTES

No more shall I behold thee.

ELECTRA

Nor shall I approach thine eye.

ORESTES

This is my last address to thee.

ELECTRA

O fare thee well, city, and fare ye well, and greatly well,
my female citizens.   1050

ORESTES

O most faithful sister, art thou now on thy way?

ELECTRA

I am on my way, bedewing my tender cheek.

ORESTES

Pylades, go rejoicing, wed the form of Electra.   1053

CASTOR and POLLUX

The marriage shall be their care; but do thou, fleeing from
these dogs, wend thy way to Athens, for with their snaky
hands, these black-skinned (Furies), fraught with the fruit
of dreadful woes, cast their dread footstep upon thee. But we
(hie) to the Sicilian Sea in haste, to save the marine prows
of ships. And passing through the ethereal plain, the wicked
indeed we aid not; but to whom holiness and justice is dear
in their life, these we preserve, releasing them from heavy
toils. Thus let no one be willing to act unjustly, nor let
him sail together with the perjured. I, a God, proclaim this
to mortals.   1063

CHORUS

Farewell; but whosoever of mortals is able to fare well,
and bends not under some misfortune, fares happily.   1064

(Exit.)

(LIGHTS FADE.)

(CURTAINS.)

(END OF PLAY.)

ORESTES

PERSONS REPRESENTED

ELECTRA

HELEN

HERMIONE

CHORUS

ORESTES

MENELAUS

TYNDARUS

PYLADES

A PHRYGIAN

APOLLO

THE ARGUMENT

Orestes, in revenge for the murder of his father, took off Aegisthus and Clytemnestra; but having dared to slay his mother, he was instantly punished for it by being afflicted with madness. But on Tyndarus, the father of her who was slain, laying an accusation against him, the Argives were about to give a public decision on this question, "What ought he, who has dared this impious deed, to suffer?" By chance Menelaus, having returned from his wanderings, sent in Helen indeed by night, but himself came by day, and being entreated by Orestes to aid him, he rather feared Tyndarus the accuser: but when the speeches came to be spoken among the populace, the multitude were stirred up to kill Orestes.

But Pylades, his friend, accompanying him, counselled him first to take revenge on Menelaus by killing Helen. As they were going on this project, they were disappointed of their hope by the Gods snatching away Helen from them. But Electra delivered up Hermione, when she made her appearance, into their hands; and they were about to kill her. When Menelaus came, and saw himself bereft by them at once of his wife and child, he endeavored to storm the palace; but they, anticipating his purpose, threatened to set it on fire. Apollo, however, having appeared, said, that he had conducted Helen to the Gods, and commanded Orestes to take Hermione to wife, and Electra to dwell with Pylades, and, after that he was purified of the murder, to reign over Argos.

SCENE: Argos.

ELECTRA

There is no word so dreadful to relate, nor suffering, nor heaven-inflicted calamity, the burden of which human nature may not be compelled to bear. For Tantalus, the blest, (and I am not reproaching his fortune, *when I say this*,) the son of Jupiter, as they report, trembling at the rock which impends over his head, hangs in the air, and suffers this punishment, as they say indeed, because, although being a man, yet having the honour of a table in common with the Gods upon equal terms, he possessed an ungovernable tongue, a most disgraceful malady. He begat Pelops, and from him sprung Atreus, for whom the Goddess having carded the wool spun the thread of contention, and doomed him to make war on Thyestes his relation; (why must I commemorate things unspeakable?) But Atreus then killed his children—and feasted him. But from Atreus, for I pass over in silence the misfortunes which intervened, sprung Agamemnon, the illustrious, (if he was indeed illustrious,) and Menelaus; their mother Aerope of Crete. But Menelaus indeed marries Helen, the hated of the Gods, but King Agamemnon obtained Clytemnestra's bed, memorable throughout the Grecians: from whom we virgins were born, three from one mother, Chrysothemis, and Iphigenia, and myself Electra; and Orestes the male part of the family, from a most unholy mother, who slew her husband, having covered him around with an inextricable robe; the reason however it is not decorous in a virgin to tell; I leave this undeclared for men to consider as they will. But why indeed must I accuse the injustice of Phoebus? Yet persuaded he Orestes to kill that mother who brought him forth, a deed which gained not a good report from all men. But nevertheless he did slay her, as he would not be disobedient to the God. I also took a share in the murder, but such as a woman ought to take. As did Pylades also who perpetrated this deed with us. From that time wasting away, the wretched Orestes is afflicted with a grievous malady, but falling on his couch there lies, but his mother's blood whirls him to frenzy (for I dread to mention those Goddesses, the Eumenides, who persecute him with terror). Moreover this is the sixth day since his slaughtered mother was purified by fire as to her body. During which he has neither taken any food down his throat, he has not bathed his limbs, but covered beneath his cloak, when indeed his body is lightened of its disease, on coming to his right mind he weeps, but at another time starts suddenly from his couch, as a colt from his yoke. But it has been decreed by this city of Argos, that no one shall receive us who have slain a mother under their roof, nor at their fire, and that none shall speak to us; but this is the appointed day, in the which the city of the Argives will pronounce their vote, whether it is fitting that we should die being stoned with stones, or having whet the sword, should plunge it into our necks. But I yet have some hope that we may not die, for Menelaus has arrived at this country from Troy, and filling the Nauplian harbor with his oars is mooring his fleet off the shore, having been lost in wanderings from Troy a long time: but the much-afflicted Helen has he sent before to our palace, having taken advantage of the night, lest any of those, whose children died under Ilium, when they saw her coming by day, might go so far as to stone her; but she is within, bewailing her sister, and the calamity of her family. She has however some consolation in her woes, for the virgin Hermione, whom Menelaus bringing from Sparta, left at our palace, when he sailed to Troy, and gave as a charge to my mother to bring up, in her she rejoices, and forgets her miseries. But I am looking at each avenue when I shall see Menelaus present, since, for the rest, we ride on slender power, if we receive not some succor from him; the house of the unfortunate is an embarrassed state of affairs.   68

ELECTRA, HELEN

HELEN

O daughter of Clytemnestra and Agamemnon, Electra, thou that hast remained a virgin a long time. How are ye, O wretched woman, both you, and your brother, the wretched Orestes (he was the murderer of his mother)? For by thy converse I am not polluted, transferring, as I do, the blame to Phoebus. And yet I groan the death of Clytemnestra, whom, after that I sailed to Troy, (how did I sail, urged by the maddening fate of the Gods!) I saw not, but of her bereft I lament my fortune.   76

ELECTRA

Helen, why should I inform thee of things thou seest thyself here present, the race of Agamemnon in calamities. I indeed sleepless sit companion to the wretched corse, (for he is a corse, in that he breathes so little,) but at his fortune I murmur not. But thou a happy woman, and thy husband a happy man, have come to us, who fare most wretchedly.   81

HELEN
But what length of time has he been lying on his couch?

ELECTRA
Ever since he shed his parent's blood.

HELEN
Oh wretched, and his mother too, that thus she perished!

ELECTRA
These things are thus, so that he is unable to speak for
misery.   85

HELEN
By the Gods wilt thou oblige me in a thing, O virgin?

ELECTRA
As far as I am permitted by the little leisure I have from
watching by my brother.

HELEN
Wilt thou go to the tomb of my sister?

ELECTRA
My mother's tomb dost thou desire? wherefore?

HELEN
Bearing the first offerings of my hair, and my libations.

ELECTRA
But is it not lawful for thee to go to the tomb of thy
friends?   91

HELEN
No, for I am ashamed to shew myself among the Argives.

ELECTRA
Late art thou discreet, then formerly leaving thine home
disgracefully.

HELEN
True hast thou spoken, but thou speakest not pleasantly to
me.

ELECTRA
But what shame possesses thee among the Myceneans?   95

HELEN
I fear the fathers of those who are dead under Ilium.

ELECTRA
For this is a dreadful thing; and at Argos thou art declaimed against by every one's mouth.

HELEN
Do thou then grant me this favor, and free me from this fear.

ELECTRA
I cannot look upon the tomb of my mother.

HELEN
And yet it is disgraceful for servants to bear these.　　100

ELECTRA
But why not send thy daughter Hermione?

HELEN
It is not well for virgins to go among the crowd.

ELECTRA
And yet she might repay the dead the care of her education.

HELEN
Right hast thou spoken, and I obey thee, virgin, and I will send my daughter, for thou sayest well. Come forth, my child Hermione, before the house, and take these libations in thine hand, and my hair, and, going to the tomb of Clytemnestra, leave there this mixture of milk and honey, and the froth of wine, and standing on the summit of the mound, say thus: "Helen, thy sister, presents thee with these libations, in fear herself to approach thy tomb, and afraid of the populace of Argos:" and bid her hold kind intentions towards me, and thyself, and my husband, and towards these two miserable persons whom the God has destroyed. But promise all the offerings to the manes, whatever it is fitting that I should perform for a sister. Go, my child, hasten, and when thou hast offered the libations at the tomb, remember to return back as speedily as possible.　　118

ELECTRA
(Alone.)
O Nature, what a great evil art thou among men, and the safeguard of those who possess thee with virtue! For see, how

she has shorn off the extremities of her hair, in order to preserve her beauty; but she is the same woman she always was. May the Gods detest thee, for that thou hast destroyed me, and this man, and the whole state of Greece: oh wretch that I am! But my dear friends that accompany me in my lamentations are again present; perhaps they will disturb the sleeper from his slumber, and will melt my eyes in tears when I behold my brother raving.   127

ELECTRA, CHORUS

ELECTRA

O most dear woman, proceed with a gentle foot, make no noise, let there be heard no sound. For your friendliness is very kind, but to awake him will be a calamity to me. Hush, hush—gently advance the tread of thy sandal, make no noise, let there be heard no sound. Move onward from that place— onward from before the couch.   132

CHORUS

Behold, I obey.

ELECTRA

St! st! Speak to me, my friend, as the breathing of the soft reed pipe.

CHORUS

See, I utter a voice low as an under note.

ELECTRA

Ay, thus come hither, come hither, approach quietly—go quietly: tell me, for what purpose, I pray, are ye come? For he has fallen on his couch, and been sleeping some time.

CHORUS

How is he? Give us an account of him, my friend.   139

ELECTRA

What fortune can I say of him? and what his calamities? still indeed he breathes, but sighs at short intervals.

CHORUS

What sayest thou? Oh, the unhappy man!

ELECTRA

You will kill him if you move his eyelids, now that he is taking the sweetest enjoyment of sleep.

CHORUS

Unfortunate on account of these most angry deeds from heaven! oh! wretched on account of thy sufferings!   144

ELECTRA

Alas! alas! Apollo himself unjust, then spoke unjust things, when at the tripod of Themis he commanded the unhallowed, inauspicious murder of my mother.   146

CHORUS

Dost thou see? he moves his body in the robes that cover him.

ELECTRA

You by your cries, O wretch, have disturbed him from his sleep.

CHORUS

I indeed think he is sleeping yet.

ELECTRA

Will you not depart from us? will you not bend your footsteps back from the house, ceasing this noise?   151

CHORUS

He sleeps.

ELECTRA

Thou sayest well.

CHORUS

Venerable, venerable Night, thou that dispensest sleep to languid mortals, come from Erebus; come, come, borne on thy wings to the house of Agamemnon; for by our griefs and by our sufferings we are quite undone, undone.   156

ELECTRA

Ye were making a noise.

CHORUS

No.

ELECTRA

Silently, silently repressing the high notes of your voice, apart from his couch, you will enable him to have the tranquil enjoyment of sleep.   160

CHORUS

Tell us; what end to his miseries awaits him?

ELECTRA

Death, death; what else can? for he has no appetite for food.

CHORUS

Death then is manifestly before him.

ELECTRA

Phoebus offered us as victims, when he commanded the dreadful, abhorred murder of our mother, that slew our father.

CHORUS

With justice indeed, but not well.   165

ELECTRA

Thou hast died, thou hast died, mother, O thou that didst bring me forth, but hast killed the father, and the children of thy blood. We perish, we perish, even as two corses. For thou art among the dead, and the greatest part of my life is past in groans, and wailings, and nightly tears; marriageless, childless, behold, how like a miserable wretch do I drag out my existence for ever!   170

CHORUS

O virgin Electra, approach near, and look that thy brother has not died unobserved by thee; for by this excessive quiet he doth not please me.   172

ORESTES, ELECTRA, CHORUS

ORESTES

O precious balm of sleep, thou that relievest my malady, how pleasant didst thou come to me in the time of need! divine oblivion of my sufferings, how wise thou art, and the goddess to be supplicated by all in distress!—whence, in heaven's name, came I hither? and how brought? For I remember not things past, bereaved, as I am, of my senses.   177

ELECTRA

My dearest brother, how didst thou delight me when thou didst fall asleep! wilt thou I touch thee, and raise thy body up?

ORESTES

Raise me then, raise me, and wipe the clotted foam from off my wretched mouth, and from my eyes.

ELECTRA

Behold, the task is sweet, and I refuse not to administer to a brother's limbs with a sister's hand.   180

ORESTES

Lay thy side by my side, and remove the squalid hair from my face, for I see but imperfectly with my eyes.

ELECTRA

O wretched head, sordid with ringlets, how art thou disordered from long want of the bath!

ORESTES

Lay me on the couch again; when my fit of madness gives me a respite, I am feeble and weak in my limbs.

ELECTRA

Behold, the couch is pleasant to the sick man, an irksome thing to keep, but still a necessary one.

ORESTES

Again raise me upright—turn my body.   185

CHORUS

Sick persons are hard to be pleased from their feebleness.

ELECTRA

Wilt thou set thy feet on the ground, putting forward thy long-discontinued step? In all things change is sweet.

ORESTES

Yes, by all means; for this has a semblance of health, but the semblance is good, though it be distant from the truth.

ELECTRA

Hear now therefore, my brother, while yet the Furies suffer thee to have thy right faculties.   190

ORESTES

Wilt thou tell any news? and if good indeed, thou art conferring pleasure; but if it pertain at all to mischief—I have enough distress.

ELECTRA

Menelaus has arrived, the brother of thy father, but his ships are moored in the Nauplian bay.

ORESTES

How sayest? Is he come, a light in mine and thy sufferings, a man of kindred blood, and that hath received benefits from our father?

ELECTRA

He is come; take this a sure proof of my words, bringing with him Helen from the walls of Troy.   195

ORESTES

Had he been saved alone, he had been more blest.
But if he brings his wife, he has arrived with a mighty evil.

ELECTRA

Tyndarus begat an offspring of daughters, a conspicuous mark for blame, and infamous throughout Greece.

ORESTES

Do thou then be unlike the bad, for it is in thy power. And not only say, but also hold these sentiments.   200

ELECTRA

Alas! my brother, thine eye rolls wildly; quick art thou changed to madness, so late in thy senses.

ORESTES

O mother, I implore thee, urge not on me those Furies gazing blood, horrid with snakes, for these, these are leaping around me.   204

ELECTRA

Remain, wretched man, calmly on thy couch, for thou seest none of those things, which thou fanciest thou seest plainly.

ORESTES

O Phoebus, these dire Goddesses in the shape of dogs will kill me, these gorgon-visaged ministers of hell.   207

ELECTRA

I will not let thee go, but, putting my arm around thee,
will stop thy starting into those unfortunate convulsions.

ORESTES

Loose me. Thou art one of my Furies, and seizest me by the
middle, that thou mayest hurl me into Tartarus.

ELECTRA

Oh! wretched me! what assistance can I obtain, since we
have on us the vengeful wrath of heaven!   210

ORESTES

Give me my bow of horn, the gift of Phoebus, with which
Apollo said I should repel the Fiends, if they appalled me by
their maddened raging.

ELECTRA

Shall any God be wounded by mortal hand?   213

ORESTES

Yes. She shall, if she will not depart from my sight Hear
ye not—see ye not the winged shafts impelled from the distant-
wounding bow? Ha! Ha! Why tarry ye yet? Skim the high air
with your wings, and impeach the oracles of Phoebus.—Ah! why
am I thus disquieted, heaving my panting breath from my lungs?
Whither, whither have I wandered from my couch? For from the
waves again I see a calm.—Sister, why weepest, hiding thine
eyes beneath thy vests, I am ashamed to have thee a partner
in my sufferings, and to give a virgin trouble through my
malady. Pine not away on account of my miseries: for thou
indeed didst assent to this, but the shedding of my mother's
blood was accomplished by me: but I blame Apollo, who, after
having instigated me to a most unholy act, with words indeed
consoled me, but not with deeds. But I think that my father,
had I, beholding him, asked him if it were right for me to
slay my mother, would have put forth many supplications,
beseeching me by this beard not to impel my sword to the
slaughter of her who bore me, if neither he thereby could be
restored to life, and I thus wretched must go through such
miseries. And now then unveil thyself, my sister, and cease
from tears, even though we be very miserable: but when thou
seest me desponding, do thou restrain my distraction, and
that which preys upon my mind, and console me; but when thou
groanest, it becomes my duty to come to thee, and suggest
words of comfort. For these are the good offices friends ought
to render each other. But go thou into the house, O

unfortunate sister, and, stretched at full length, compose thy sleepless eyelids to sleep, and take refreshment, and pour the bath upon thy fair skin. For if thou forsakest me, or gettest any illness by continually sitting by me, we perish; for thee I have my only succor, by the rest, as thou seest, abandoned. 244

ELECTRA

This cannot be: with thee will I choose to die, with thee to live; for it is the same: for if thou shouldest die, what can I do, a woman? how shall I be preserved, alone and destitute? without a brother, without a father, without a friend: but if it seemeth good to thee, these things it is my duty to do: but recline thy body on the bed, and do not to such a degree conceive to be real whatever frightens and startles thee from the couch, but keep quiet on the bed strewn for thee. For though thou be not ill, but only seem to be ill, still this even is an evil and a distress to mortals.

CHORUS

Alas! alas! swift-winged, raving Goddesses, who keep up the dance, not that of Bacchus, with tears and groans. You, dark Eumenides, you, that fly through the wide extended air, executing vengeance, executing slaughter, you do I supplicate, I supplicate: suffer the offspring of Agamemnon to forget his furious madness; alas! for his sufferings. What were they that eagerly grasping at, thou unhappy perishest, having received from the tripod the oracle which Phoebus spake, on that pavement, where are said to be the recesses in the midst of the globe! O Jupiter, what pity is there? what is this contention of slaughter that comes persecuting thee wretched, to whom some evil genius casts tear upon tear, transporting to thy house the blood of thy mother which drives thee frenzied! Thus I bewail, I bewail. Great prosperity is not lasting among mortals; but, as the sail of the swift bark, some deity having shaken him, hath sunk him in the voracious and destructive waves of tremendous evils, as in the waves of the ocean. For what other family ought I to reverence yet before that sprung from divine nuptials, sprung from Tantalus?—But lo! the king! the prince Menelaus, is coming! but he is very easily discernible from the elegance of his person, as king of the house of the Tantalidae. O thou that didst direct the army of a thousand vessels to Asia's land, hail! but thou comest hither with good fortune, having obtained the object of thy wishes from the Gods. 278

MENELAUS, ORESTES, CHORUS

MENELAUS

O palace, in some respect indeed I behold thee with pleasure, coming from Troy, but in other respect I groan when I see thee. For never yet saw I any other house more completely encircled round with lamentable woes. For I was made acquainted with the misfortune that befell Agamemnon, (and his death, by what death he perished at the hands of his wife,) when I was landing my ships at Malea; but from the waves the prophet of the mariners declared unto me, the foreboding Glaucus the son of Nereus, an unerring God, who told me thus in evident form standing by me. "Menelaus, thy brother lieth dead, having fallen in his last bath, which his wife prepared." But he filled both me and my sailors with many tears; but when I come to the Nauplian shore, my wife having already landed there, expecting to clasp in my friendly embraces Orestes the son of Agamemnon, and his mother, as being in prosperity, I heard from some fisherman the unhallowed murder of the daughter of Tyndarus. And now tell me, maidens, where is the son of Agamemnon, who dared these terrible deeds of evil? for he was an infant in Clytemnestra's arms at that time when I left the palace on my way to Troy, so that I should not know him, were I to see him.   298

ORESTES

I, Menelaus, am Orestes, whom thou seekest, I of my own accord will declare my evils. But first I touch thy knees in supplication, putting up prayers from my mouth, not using the sacred branch: save me. But thou art come in the very season of my sufferings.   302

MENELAUS

O ye Gods, what do I behold! whom of the dead do I see!

ORESTES

Ay! well thou sayest the dead; for in my state of suffering I live not; but see the light.

MENELAUS

Thou wretched man, how disordered thou art in thy squalid hair!   305

ORESTES

Not the appearance, but the deeds torment me.

MENELAUS
But thou glarest dreadfully with thy shriveled eyeballs.

ORESTES
My body is vanished, but my name has not left me.

MENELAUS
Alas, thy uncomeliness of form which has appeared to me beyond conception!

ORESTES
I am he, the murderer of my wretched mother.   310

MENELAUS
I have heard; but spare a little the recital of thy woes.

ORESTES
I spare it; but in woes the deity is rich to me.

MENELAUS
What dost thou suffer? What malady destroys thee?

ORESTES
The conviction that I am conscious of having perpetrated dreadful deeds.   314

MENELAUS
How sayest thou? Plainness, and not obscurity, is wisdom.

ORESTES
Sorrow is chiefly what destroys me,—

MENELAUS
She is a dreadful goddess, but sorrow admits of cure.

ORESTES
And fits of madness in revenge for my mother's blood.

MENELAUS
But when didst first have the raging? what day was it then?

ORESTES
That day in which I heaped the tomb on my mother.   320

MENELAUS
What? in the house, or sitting at the pyre?

ORESTES

As I was guarding by night lest any one should bear off her bones.

MENELAUS

Was any one else present, who supported thy body?

ORESTES

Pylades, who perpetrated with me the vengeance and death of my mother.

MENELAUS

But by what visions art thou thus afflicted? 325

ORESTES

I appear to behold three virgins like the night.

MENELAUS

I know whom thou meanest, but am unwilling to name them.

ORESTES

Yes: for they are awful; but forbear from speaking such high polished words.

MENELAUS

Do these drive thee to distraction on account of this kindred murder?

ORESTES

Alas me for the persecutions, with which wretched I am driven! 330

MENELAUS

It is not strange that those who do strange deeds should suffer them.

ORESTES

But we have whereto we may transfer the criminality of the mischance.

MENELAUS

Say not the death *of thy father*; for this is not wise.

ORESTES

Phoebus who commanded us to perpetrate the slaying of our mother. 334

MENELAUS
Being more ignorant than to know equity, and justice.

ORESTES
We are servants of the Gods, whatever those Gods be.

MENELAUS
And then does not Apollo assist thee in thy miseries?

ORESTES
He is always about to do it, but such are the Gods
by nature.

MENELAUS
But how long a time has thy mother's breath gone from her?

ORESTES
This is the sixth day since; the funeral pyre is yet warm.

MENELAUS
How quickly have the Goddesses come to demand of thee thy
mother's blood!   341

ORESTES
I am not wise, but a true friend to my friends.

MENELAUS
But what then doth the revenge of thy father profit thee?

ORESTES
Nothing yet; but I consider what is in prospect in the same
light as a thing not done.

MENELAUS
But regarding the city how standest thou, having done these
things?   345

ORESTES
We are hated to that degree, that no one speaks to us.

MENELAUS
Nor hast thou washed thy blood from thy hands according to
the laws?

ORESTES
How can I? for I am shut out from the houses, whithersoever
I go.

MENELAUS
Who of the citizens thus contend to drive thee from the land?

ORESTES
Oeax, imputing to my father the hatred which arose on account of Troy.   350

MENELAUS
I understand. The death of Palamede takes its vengeance on thee.

ORESTES
In which at least I had no share—but I perish by the three.

MENELAUS
But who else? Is it perchance one of the friends of Aegisthus?

ORESTES
They persecute me, whom now the city obeys.   354

MENELAUS
But does the city suffer thee to wield Agamemnon's sceptre?

ORESTES
How should they? who no longer suffer us to live.

MENELAUS
Doing what, which thou canst tell me as a clear fact?

ORESTES
This very day sentence will be passed upon us.

MENELAUS
To be exiled from this city? or to die? or not to die?

ORESTES
To die, by being stoned with stones by the citizens.   360

MENELAUS
And dost thou not fly then, escaping beyond the boundaries of the country?

ORESTES
How can we? for we are surrounded on every side by brazen arms.

MENELAUS
By private enemies, or by the hand of Argos?   363

ORESTES
By all the citizens, that I may die—the word is brief.

MENELAUS
O unhappy man! thou art come to the extreme of misfortune.

ORESTES
On thee my hope builds her escape from evils, but, thyself
happy, coming among the distressed, impart thy good fortune
to thy friends, and be not the only man to retain a benefit
thou hast received, but undertake also services in thy turn,
paying their father's kindness to those to whom thou oughtest.
For those friends have the name, not the reality, who are not
friends in adversity.   371

CHORUS
And see the Spartan Tyndarus is toiling hither with his
aged foot, in a black vest, and shorn, his locks cut off in
mourning for his daughter.

ORESTES
I am undone, O Menelaus! Lo! Tyndarus is coming towards
us, to come before whose presence, most of all men's, shame
covereth me, on account of what has been done. For he used to
nurture me when I was little, and satiated me with many
kisses, dandling in his arms Agamemnon's boy, and Leda with
him, honoring me no less than the twin-born of Jove. For
which, my wretched heart and soul, I have given no good
return: what dark veil can I take for my countenance? what
cloud can I place before me, that I may avoid the glances of
the old man's eyes?   382

TYNDARUS, MENELAUS, ORESTES, CHORUS

TYNDARUS
Where, where can I see my daughter's husband Menelaus? For
as I was pouring my libations on the tomb of Clytemnestra, I
heard that he was come to Nauplia with his wife, safe through
a length of years. Conduct me, for I long to stand by his
hand and salute him, seeing my friend after a long lapse of
time.   387

MENELAUS
O hail! old man, who sharest thy bed with Jove.

TYNDARUS

O hail! thou also, Menelaus my dear relation,—ah! what an evil is it not to know the future! This dragon here, the murderer of his mother, glares before the house his pestilential gleams—the object of my detestation—Menelaus, dost thou speak to this unholy wretch?   392

MENELAUS

Why not? he is the son of a father who was dear to me.

TYNDARUS

What! was he sprung from him, being such as he is?

MENELAUS

He was; but, though he be unfortunate, he should be respected.   395

TYNDARUS

Having been a long time with barbarians, thou art thyself turned barbarian.

MENELAUS

Nay! it is the Grecian fashion always to honour one of kindred blood.

TYNDARUS

Yes, and also not to wish to be above the laws.

MENELAUS

Every thing proceeding from necessity is considered as subservient to her among the wise.

TYNDARUS

Do thou then keep to this, but I'll have none of it.   400

MENELAUS

No, for anger joined with thine age, is not wisdom.

TYNDARUS

With this man what controversy can there be regarding wisdom? If what things are virtuous, and what are not virtuous, are plain to all, what man was ever more unwise than this man? who did not indeed consider justice, nor applied to the common existing law of the Grecians. For after that Agamemnon breathed forth his last, struck by my daughter on the head, a most foul deed (for never will I approve of this), it behooved him indeed to lay against her a sacred charge of bloodshed, following up the accusation, and to cast his mother from out of the house; and he would have taken the wise side in the calamity, and would have kept to law, and would have been pious. But now has he come to the same fate with his mother. For with justice thinking her wicked, himself has become more wicked in slaying his mother.   414

But thus much, Menelaus, will I ask thee; If the wife that shared his bed were to kill him, and his son again kills his mother in return, and he that is born of him shall expiate the murder with murder, whither then will the extremes of these evils proceed? Well did our fathers of old lay down these things; they suffered not him to come into the sight of their eyes, not to their converse, who was under an attainder of blood; but they made him atone by banishment; they suffered however none to kill him in return. For always were one about to be attainted of murder, taking the pollution last into his hands. But I hate indeed impious women, but first among them my daughter, who slew her husband. But never will I approve of Helen thy wife, nor would I speak to her, neither do I commend I thee for going to the plain of Troy on account of a perfidious woman. But I will defend the law, as far at least as I am able, putting a stop to this brutish and murderous practice, which is ever destructive both of the country and the state.—For what feelings of humanity hadst thou, thou wretched man, when she bared her breast in supplication, thy mother? I indeed, though I witnessed not that scene of misery, melt in my aged eyes with tears through wretchedness. One thing however goes to the scale of my arguments; thou art both hated by the Gods, and sufferest vengeance of thy mother, wandering about with madness and terrors; why must I hear by the testimony of others, what it is in my power to see? That thou mayest know then once for all, Menelaus, do not things contrary to the Gods, through thy wishes to assist this man. But suffer him to be slain by the citizens with stones, or set not thy foot on Spartan ground. But my daughter in dying met with justice, but it was not fitting that she should die by him . In other respects indeed have I been a happy man, except in my daughters, but in this I am not happy.   445

CHORUS

He is enviable, who is fortunate in his children, and has not on him notorious calamities.

ORESTES

O old man, I tremble to speak to thee, wherein I am about to grieve thee and thy mind. But I am unholy in that I slew my mother; but holy at least in another point of view, having avenged my father. Let then thine age, which hinders me through fear from speaking, be removed out of the way of my words, and I will go on in a direct path; but now do I fear thy grey hairs. What could I do? for oppose the facts, two against two. My father indeed begat me, but thy daughter brought me forth, a field receiving the seed from another; but without a father there never could be a child. I reasoned therefore with myself, that I should assist the prime author of my birth rather than the aliment which under him produced me. But thy daughter (I am ashamed to call her mother), in secret and unchaste nuptials, had approached the bed of another man; of myself, if I speak ill of her, shall I be speaking, but yet will I tell it. Aegisthus was her secret husband in her palace. Him I slew, and after him I sacrificed my mother, doing indeed unholy things, but avenging my father. But as touching those things for which thou threatenest that I must be stoned, hear, how I shall assist all Greece. For if the women shall arrive at such a pitch of boldness as to murder the men, making good their escape with regard to their children, seeking to captivate their pity by their breasts, it would be as nothing with them to slay their husbands, having any pretext that might chance; but I having done dreadful things (as thou sayest), have put a stop to this law, but hating my mother deservedly I slew her, who betrayed her husband absent from home in arms, the generalissimo of the whole land of Greece, and kept not her bed undefiled. But when she perceived that she had done amiss, she inflicted not vengeance on herself, but, that she might not suffer vengeance from her husband, punished and slew my father. By the Gods, (in no good cause have I named the Gods, pleading against a charge of murder,) had I by my silence praised my mother's actions, what then would the deceased have done to me? To my mother indeed the Furies are present as allies, but would they not be present to him, who has received the greater injury? Would he not, detesting me, have haunted me with the Furies? Thou then, old man, by begetting a bad daughter, hast destroyed me; for through her boldness deprived of my father, I became a matricide. Dost see? Telemachus slew not the wife of Ulysses, for she married not a husband on a husband, but her marriage bed remains unpolluted in the palace. Dost see? Apollo, who, dwelling in his habitation in the midst of the earth, gives the most clear oracles to mortals, by whom we are entirely guided, whatever he may say, on him relying slew I my mother. 'Twas he who erred, not I: what could I do? Is not the God sufficient for me, who transfer *the deed* to him, to do away with the pollution? Whither then can any fly for succor, unless he that commanded me shall deliver me from death? But say not these things have been done "not well;" but *say* "not fortunately" for us who did them. But to whatsoever men their marriages are well established, there is a happy life, but to those to whom they fall not out well, with regard to their affairs both at home and abroad they are unfortunate.   501

CHORUS

Women were born always to be in the way of what may happen to men, to the making of things unfortunate.

TYNDARUS

Since thou art bold, and yieldest not to my speech, but thus answerest me so as to grieve my mind, thou wilt rather inflame me to urge thy death. But this I shall consider a handsome addition to those labors for which I came, *namely*, to deck my daughter's tomb. For going to the multitude of the Argives assembled, I will rouse the state willing and not unwilling, to pass the sentence of being stoned on thee and on thy sister; but she is worthy of death rather than thee, who irritated thee against her mother, always pealing in thine ear words to increase thy hatred, relating dreams she had of Agamemnon, and this also, that the infernal Gods detested the bed of Aegisthus; for even here on earth it were hard *to be endured*; until she set the house in flames with fire more strong than Vulcan's.—Menelaus, but to thee I speak this, and will moreover perform it. If thou regard my hate, and my alliance, ward not off death from this man in opposition to the Gods; but suffer him to be slain by the citizens with stones, or set not thy foot on Spartan ground. Thus much having heard, depart, nor choose the impious for thy friends, passing over the pious.—But O attendants, conduct us from this house.   522

ORESTES

Depart, that the remainder of my speech may reach this man uninterrupted by the clamors of thy age: Menelaus, whither dost thou roam in thought, entering on a double path of double care?   525

MENELAUS

Suffer me; having some thoughts within myself, I am perplexed to which side of fortune to turn me.

ORESTES

Do not make up thy opinion, but having first heard my words, then deliberate.

MENELAUS

Say on; for thou hast spoken rightly; but there are seasons where silence may be better than talking, and there are seasons where talking may be better than silence.   529

ORESTES

I will speak then forthwith: Long speeches have the preference before short ones, and are more plain to hear. Give thou to me nothing of what thou hast, O Menelaus, but what thou hast received from my father, return; I mean not riches—yet riches, which are the most dear of what I possess, if thou wilt preserve my life. Say I am unjust, I ought to receive from thee, instead of this evil, something contrary to what justice demands; for Agamemnon my father having collected Greece in arms, in a way justice did not demand, went to Troy, not having erred himself, but in order to set right the error, and injustice of thy wife. This one thing indeed thou oughtest to give me for one thing, but he, as friends should for friends, of a truth exposed his person for thee toiling at the shield, that thou mightest receive back thy wife. Repay me then this kindness for that which thou receivedst there, toiling for one day in standing as my succor, not completing ten years. But the sacrifice of my sister, which Aulis received, this I suffer thee to have; do not kill Hermione, *I ask it not*. For, I being in the state in which I now am, thou must of necessity have the advantage, and I must suffer it to be so. But grant my life to my wretched father, and my sister's, who has been a virgin a lung time. For dying I shall leave ray father's house destitute. Thou wilt say "impossible:" this is the very thing *I have been urging*, it behooves friends to help their friends in misfortunes. But when the God gives prosperity, what need is there of friends? For the God himself sufficeth, being willing to assist. Thou appearest to all the Greeks to be fond of thy wife; (and this I say, not stealing under thee imperceptibly with flattery;) by her I implore thee; O wretched me for my woes, to what have I come? but why must I suffer thus? For in behalf of the whole house I make this supplication. divine brother of my father, conceive that the dead man beneath the earth hears these things, and that his spirit is hovering over thee, and speaks what I speak. These things have I said, with tears, and groans, and miseries, and have prayed earnestly, looking for preservation, which all, and not I only seek.   566

CHORUS

I too implore thee, although a woman, yet still I implore thee to succor those in need, but thou art able.

MENELAUS

Orestes, I indeed reverence thy person, and I am willing to labor with thee in thy misfortunes. For thus it is right to endure together the misfortunes of one's relations, if the God gives the ability, even so far as to die, and to kill the adversary; but this ability again I want from the Gods. For I am come having my single spear unaided by allies, having wandered with infinite labors with small assistance of friends left me. In battle therefore we cannot come off superior to Pelasgian Argos; but if we can by soft speeches, to that hope are we equal. For how can any one achieve great actions with small means? For when the rabble is in full force falling into a rage, it is equally difficult to extinguish as a fierce fire. But if one quietly yields to it as it is spreading, and gives in to it, watching well his opportunity, perhaps it may spend its rage, but when it has remitted from its blast, you may without difficulty have it your own way, as much as you please. For there is inherent in them pity, but there is inherent also vehement passion, to one who carefully watches his opportunity a most excellent advantage. But I will go and endeavor to persuade Tyndarus, and the city, to use their great power in a becoming manner. For a ship, the main sheet stretched out to a violent degree, is wont to pitch, but stands upright again, if you slacken the main sheet. For the God hates too great vehemence, and the citizens hate it; but I must (I speak as I mean) save thee by wisdom, not by opposing my superiors. But I cannot by force, as perchance thou thinkest, preserve thee; for it is no easy matter to erect from one single spear trophies from the evils, which are about thee. For never have we approached the land of Argos by way of supplication; but now there is necessity for the wise to become the slaves of fortune. 597

ORESTES, CHORUS

ORESTES

O thou, a mere cipher in other things except in warring for the sake of a woman; O thou most base in avenging thy friends, dost thou fly, turning away from me? But all Agamemnon's services are gone: thou wert then without friends, my father, in thy affliction. Alas me! I am betrayed, and there no longer are any hopes, whither turning I may escape death from the Argives. For he was the refuge of my safety.—But I see this most dear of men, Pylades, coming with hasty step from the Phocians, a pleasing sight, a man faithful in adversity, more grateful to behold than the calm to the mariners.

607

PYLADES, ORESTES, CHORUS

PYLADES

I came through the city with a quicker step than I ought, having heard of the council of state assembled, and seeing it plainly myself, against thee and thy sister, as about to kill you instantly.—What is this? how art thou? in what state, O most dear to me of my companions and kindred? for all these things art thou to me.

612

ORESTES

We are gone—briefly to shew thee my calamities.

PYLADES

Thou wilt have ruined me too; for the things of friends are common.

ORESTES

Menelaus has behaved most basely towards me and my sister.

PYLADES

It is to be expected that the husband of a bad wife be bad.

ORESTES

He is come, and has done just as much for me as if he had not come.

616

PYLADES

What! is he in truth come to this land?

ORESTES

After a long season; but nevertheless he was very soon discovered to be too base to his friends.

PYLADES

And has he brought in his ship with him his most infamous wife?

ORESTES

Not he her, but she brought him hither.

620

PYLADES

Where is she, who, beyond any woman, destroyed most of the Grecians?

ORESTES

In my palace, if I may indeed be allowed to call this mine.

PYLADES

But what words didst thou say to thy father's brother?

ORESTES

I requested him not to suffer me and my sister to be slain by the citizens.

PYLADES

By the Gods, what said he to this request; this I wish to know.   625

ORESTES

He declined, from motives of prudence, as bad friends act towards their friends.

PYLADES

Going on what ground of excuse? This having learnt, I am in possession of every thing.

ORESTES

The father himself came, he that begat such excellent daughters.

PYLADES

Tyndarus you mean; perhaps enraged with thee on account of his daughter.

ORESTES

You are right: he paid more attention to his ties with him, than to his ties with my father.   630

PYLADES

And dared he not, being present, to take arms against thy troubles?

ORESTES

No: for he was not born a warrior, but brave among women.

                    PYLADES
    Thou art then in the greatest miseries, and it is necessary
for thee to die.   634

                    ORESTES
    The citizens must pass their vote on us for the murder we
have committed.

                    PYLADES
    Which vote what will it decide? tell me, for I am in fear.

                    ORESTES
    Either to die or live; not many words on matters of great
import.

                    PYLADES
    Come fly, and quit the palace with thy sister.   638

                    ORESTES
    Seest thou not? we are watched by guards on every side.

                    PYLADES
    I saw the streets of the city lined with arms.   640

                    ORESTES
    We are invested as to our persons, as a city by the enemy.

                    PYLADES
    Now ask me also, what I suffer; for I too am undone.

                    ORESTES
    By whom? This would be an evil added to my evils.

                    PYLADES
    Strophius, my father, being enraged, hath driven me an
exile from his house.

                    ORESTES
    Bringing against thee some private charge, or one in common
with the citizens?   645

                    PYLADES
    Because I perpetrated with thee the murder of thy mother,
he banished me, calling me unholy.

ORESTES

O thou unfortunate! it seems that thou also sufferest for
my evils.

PYLADES

We have not Menelaus's manners—this must be borne.

ORESTES

Dost thou not fear lest Argos should wish to kill thee, as
it does also me?

PYLADES

We do not belong to these to punish, but to the land of
the Phocians.   650

ORESTES

The populace is a terrible thing, when they have evil
leaders.

PYLADES

But when they have good ones, they always deliberate good
things.

ORESTES

Be it so: we must speak on our common business.

PYLADES

On what affair of necessity?

ORESTES

Supposing I should go to the citizens, and say—   655

PYLADES

—that thou hast acted justly?

ORESTES

Ay, avenging my father:

PYLADES

I fear they might not receive thee gladly.

ORESTES

But shall I die then shuddering in silence?

PYLADES

This were cowardly.   660

ORESTES
How then can I do?

PYLADES
Hast thou any chance of safety, if thou remainest?

ORESTES
I have none.

PYLADES
But going, is there any hope of thy being preserved from
thy miseries?

ORESTES
Should it chance well, there might be.   665

PYLADES
Is not this then better than remaining?

ORESTES
Shall I go then?

PYLADES
Dying thus, at least thou wilt die more honorably.

ORESTES
And I have a just cause.

PYLADES
Only pray for its appearing so.   670

ORESTES
Thou sayest well: this way I avoid the imputation of
cowardice.

PYLADES
More than by tarrying here.

ORESTES
And some one perchance may pity me—

PYLADES
Yes; for thy nobleness of birth is a great thing.

ORESTES
—indignant at my father's death.   675

PYLADES

All this in prospect.

ORESTES

Go I must, for it is not manly to die ingloriously.

PYLADES

These sentiments I praise.

ORESTES

Shall we then tell these things to my sister?

PYLADES

No, by the Gods.   680

ORESTES

Why, there might be tears.

PYLADES

This then is a great omen.

ORESTES

Clearly it is better to be silent.

PYLADES

Thou art a gainer by delay.

ORESTES

This one thing only opposes me.   685

PYLADES

What new thing again is this thou sayest?

ORESTES

I fear lest the goddesses should stop me with their
torments.

PYLADES

But I will take care of thee.

ORESTES

It is a difficult and dangerous task to touch a man thus
disordered.

PYLADES

Not for me to touch thee.   690

ORESTES
Take care how thou art partner of my madness.

PYLADES
Let not this be thought of.

ORESTES
Wilt thou not then be timid to assist me?

PYLADES
No, for timidity is a great evil to friends.

ORESTES
Go on now, the helm of my foot.   695

PYLADES
Having a charge worthy of a friend.

ORESTES
And guide me to my father's tomb.

PYLADES
To what end is this?

ORESTES
That I may supplicate him to save me.

PYLADES
This at least is just.   700

ORESTES
But let me not see my mother's monument.

PYLADES
For she was an enemy. But hasten, that the decree of the
Argives condemn thee not before thou goest; leaning thy side,
weary with disease, on mine: since I will conduct thee through
the city, little caring for the multitude, nothing ashamed;
for where shall I shew myself thy friend, if I assist thee
not when thou art in perilous condition?   707

ORESTES
This it is to have companions, not relationship alone; so
that a man who is congenial in manners, though a stranger in
blood, is a better friend for a man to have, than ten thousand
relatives.   710

CHORUS

The great happiness, and the valor high sounding throughout Greece, and by the channels of the Simois, has again withdrawn from the fortune of the Atridae, as of old, from the ancient calamity of the house, when the strife of the golden lamb arose among the descendants of Tantalus; most shocking feasts, and the slaughter of noble children; from whence murder responsive to murder fails not to attend on the two sons of Atreus. What seems good is not good, to gash the parents' skin with a fierce hand, and brandish the sword black-stained with blood in the sunbeams. But, on the other hand, to act wickedly is mad impiety, and the folly of evil-minded men. ₇₂₁

But the wretched daughter of Tyndarus in the fear of death shrieked out, "My son thou darest impious deeds, killing thy mother; do not, attending to the gratification of thy father, kindle an everlasting disgrace." ₇₂₄

What malady, or what tears, or what pity on earth is greater, than to imbrue one's hand in a mother's blood? What a deed, what a deed having performed, does the son of Agamemnon rave with madness, a prey to the Eumenides, marked for death, giddy with his rolling eyes! O wretched on account of his mother, when though seeing the breast bared from the robe of golden texture, he stabbed the mother in retaliation for the father's sufferings. ₇₃₁

ELECTRA, CHORUS

ELECTRA

Ye virgins, has the wretched Orestes, overcome with heaven-inflicted madness, rushed any where from this house?

CHORUS

By no means; but he is gone to the Argive people, to undergo the trial proposed regarding life, by which you must either live or die. ₇₃₄

ELECTRA

Alas me! what thing has he done? but who persuaded him?

CHORUS

Pylades.—But this messenger seems soon about to inform us of what has passed there concerning thy brother. ₇₃₆

MESSENGER, ELECTRA, CHORUS

MESSENGER

O wretched hapless daughter of the chief Agamemnon, revered Electra, hear the unfortunate words which I am come to bring.

ELECTRA

Alas! alas! we are undone; this thou signifiest by thy speech. For thou comest, as it seems, a messenger of woes.

MESSENGER

It has been carried by the vote of the Pelasgians, that thy brother and thou must die this day.   739

ELECTRA

Ah me! the expected event has come, which long since fearing, I pined away with lamentations on account of what was in prospect.—But what was the debate? What arguments amongst the Argives condemned us, and confirmed our sentence of death? Tell me, old man, whether by the hand raised to stone me, or by the sword must I breathe out my soul, having this calamity in common with my brother?   745

MESSENGER

I chanced indeed to be entering the gates from the country, anxious to hear both what regarded thee, and what regarded Orestes; for at all times I had a favorable inclination towards thy father: and thy house fed me, poor indeed, but noble in my conduct towards friends. But I see the crowd going and sitting down on an eminence; where they say Danaus first collected the people to a common council, when he suffered punishment at the hands of Aegyptus. But seeing this concourse, I asked one of the citizens, "What new thing is stirring in Argos? Has any message from hostile powers roused the city of the Danaids?" But he said, "Seest thou not this Orestes walking near us, who is about to run in the contest of life and death?" But I see an unexpected sight, which oh that I had never seen! Pylades and thy brother walking together, the one indeed broken with sickness, but the other, like a brother, sympathizing with his friend, tending his weakened state with fostering care. But when the assembly of the Argives was full, a herald stood forth and said, "Who wishes to speak on the question, whether it is right that Orestes, who has killed his mother, should die, or not?" And on this Talthybius rises, who, in conjunction with thy father, laid waste the Phrygians. But he spoke words of divided import, being the constant slave of those in power; struck

with admiration indeed at thy father, but not commending thy
brother (speciously mixing up words of bad import), because
he laid down no good laws towards his parents: but he was
continually casting a smiling glance on Aegisthus's friends.
For such is this kind; heralds always dance attendance on the
prosperous; but that man is their friend, whoever may chance
to have power in the state, and to be in office.   775
  But next to him prince Diomed harangued; he indeed was for
suffering them to kill neither thee nor thy brother, but *bid
them* observe piety by punishing you with banishment. But some
indeed murmured their assent, that he spoke well, but others
praised him not . And after him rises up some man, intemperate
in speech, powerful in boldness, an Argive, yet not an Argive
, forced upon us, relying both on the tumult, and on ignorant
boldness, prompt by persuasion to involve them in some
mischief. (For when a man, sweet in words, holding bad
sentiments, persuades the multitude, it is a great evil to
the city. But as many as always advise good things with
understanding, although not at the present moment, eventually
are of service to the state: but the intelligent leader ought
to look to this, for the case is the same with the man who
speaks words, and the man who approves them.) Who said, that
they ought to kill Orestes and thee by stoning. But Tyndarus
was privily making up such sort of speeches for him who wished
your death to speak. But another man stood up, and spoke in
opposition to him, in form indeed not made to catch the eye;
but a man endued with the qualities of a man, rarely polluting
the city, and the circle of the forum; one who farmed his own
land , which class of persons alone preserve the country, but
prudent, and wishing the tenor of his conduct to be in unison
with his words, uncorrupted, one that had conformed to a
blameless mode of living; he proposed to crown Orestes the
son of Agamemnon, who was willing to avenge his father by
slaying a wicked and unholy woman, who took this out of the
power of men, and would no one have been the cause of arming
the hand for war, nor undertaking an expedition, leaving his
home, if those who are left destroy what is entrusted to their
charge in the house, disgracing their husbands' beds. And to
right-minded men at least he appeared to speak well: and none
spoke besides, but thy brother advanced and said, "O
inhabitants of the land of Inachus, avenging you no less than
my father, I slew my mother, for if the murder of men shall
become licensed to women, ye no longer can escape dying, or
ye must be slaves to your wives. But ye do the contrary to
what ye ought to do. For now she that was false to the bed of
my father is dead; but if ye do indeed slay me, the law has

lost its force, and no man can escape dying, forasmuch as there will be no lack of this audacity."   815

But he persuaded not the people, though appearing to speak well. But that villain, who spoke among the multitude, overcomes him, he that harangued for the killing of thy brother and thee. But scarcely did the wretched Orestes persuade them that he might not die by stoning; but he promised that this day he would quit his life by self-slaughter together with thee:—but Pylades is conducting him from the council, weeping: but his friends accompany him bewailing him, pitying him; but he is coming a sad spectacle to thee, and a wretched sight. But prepare the sword, or the noose for thy neck, for thou must die, but thy nobleness of birth hath profited thee nothing, nor the Pythian Phoebus who sits on the tripod, but hath destroyed thee.   827

CHORUS

O unhappy virgin! how art thou dumb, casting thy muffled countenance towards the ground, as though about to run into a strain of groans and lamentations!   829

ELECTRA

I begin the lament, O land of Greece, digging my white nail into my cheek, sad bleeding woe, and dashing my head, which the lovely goddess of the manes beneath the earth has to her share. And let the Cyclopian land howl, applying the steel to their head cropped of hair over the calamity of our house. This pity, this pity, proceeds for those who are about to die, who once were the princes of Greece. For it is gone, it is gone, the entire race of the children of Pelops has perished, and the happiness which once resided in these blest abodes. Envy from heaven has now seized it, and the harsh decree of blood in the state. Alas! alas! O race of mortals that endure for a day, full of tears, full of troubles, behold how contrary to expectation fate comes. But in the long lapse of time each different man receives by turns his different sufferings. But the whole race of mortals is unstable and uncertain.   844

Oh! could I go to that rock stretched from Olympus in its loftiness midst heaven and earth by golden chains, that mass of clay borne round with rapid revolutions, that in my plaints I might cry out to my ancient father Tantalus; who begat the progenitors of my family, who saw calamities, what time in the pursuing of steeds, Pelops in his car drawn by four horses perpetrated, as he drove, the murder of Myrtilus, *by casting him* into the sea, hurling him down to the surge of the ocean, as he guided his car on the shore of the briny sea by Geraestus foaming with its white billows. Whence the baleful curse came on my house since, by the agency of Maia's son , there appeared the pernicious, pernicious prodigy of the golden-fleeced lamb, a birth which took place among the flocks of the warlike Atreus. On which both Discord drove back the winged chariot of the sun, directing it from the path of heaven leading to the west towards Aurora borne on her single horse . And Jupiter drove back the course of the seven moving Pleiads another way: and from that period he sends deaths in succession to deaths, and "the feast of Thyestes," so named from Thyestes. And the bed of the Cretan Aerope deceitful in a deceitful marriage has come as a finishing stroke on me and my father, to the miserable destruction of our family.   865

CHORUS

But see, thy brother is advancing, condemned by the vote of death, and Pylades the most faithful of all, a man like a brother, supporting the enfeebled limbs of Orestes, walking by his side with the foot of tender solicitude.   868

ELECTRA, ORESTES, PYLADES, CHORUS

ELECTRA

Alas me! for I bewail thee, my brother, seeing thee before the tomb, and before the pyre of thy departed shade: alas me! again and again, how am I bereft of my senses, seeing with my eyes the very last sight of thee.   871

ORESTES

Wilt thou not in silence, ceasing from womanish groans, make up thy mind to what is decreed? These things indeed are lamentable, but yet we must bear our present fate.

ELECTRA

And how can I be silent? We wretched no longer are permitted to view this light of the God.

ORESTES

Do not thou kill me; I, the unhappy, have died enough already under the hands of the Argives; but pass over our present ills.   876

ELECTRA

O Orestes! oh wretched in thy youth, and thy fate, and thy untimely death, then oughtest thou to live, when thou art no more.

ORESTES

Do not by the Gods throw cowardice around me, bringing the remembrance of my woes so as to cause tears.

ELECTRA

We shall die; it is not possible not to groan our misfortunes; for the dear life is a cause of pity to all mortals.   882

ORESTES

This is the day appointed for us! but we must either fit the suspended noose, or whet the sword with our hand.

ELECTRA

Do thou then kill me, my brother; let none of the Argives kill me, putting a contumely on the offspring of Agamemnon.

ORESTES

I have enough of thy mother's blood, but thee I will not slay; but die by thine own hand in whatever manner thou wilt.

ELECTRA

These things shall be; I will not be deserted by thy sword; but I wish to clasp my hands around thy neck.   886

ORESTES

Thou enjoyest a vain gratification, if this be an enjoyment, to throw thy hands around those who are hard at death's door.

ELECTRA

Oh thou most dear! oh thou that hast the desirable and most sweet name, and one soul with thy sister!   889

ORESTES

Thou wilt melt me; and still I wish to answer thee in the endearment of encircling arms, for why am I any longer ashamed? bosom of my sister, O dear object of my caresses, these embraces are allowed to us miserable beings instead of children and the bridal bed.   893

ELECTRA

Alas! How can the same sword (if this request be lawful) kill us, and one tomb wrought of cedar receive us?

ORESTES
This would be most sweet; but thou seest how destitute we are, in respect to being able to share our sepulture.   895

ELECTRA
Did not Menelaus speak in behalf of thee, taking a decided part against thy death, the base man, the deserter of my father?

ORESTES
He shewed it not even in his countenance, but keeping his hopes on the sceptre, he was cautious how he saved his friends. But let be, he will die acting in a manner nobly, and most worthily of Agamemnon. And I indeed will shew my high descent to the city, striking home to my heart with the sword; but thee, on the other hand, it behooveth to act in concert with my bold attempts. But do thou, Pylades, be the umpire of our death, and well compose the bodies of us when dead, and bury us together, bearing us to our father's tomb. And farewell—but I am going to the deed, as thou seest.

PYLADES
Hold. This one thing indeed first I bring in charge against thee—Dost thou think that I can wish to live when thou diest?

ORESTES
For how does it concern thee to die with me?   910

PYLADES
Dost ask? But how does it to live without thy company?

ORESTES
Thou didst not slay my mother, as I did, a wretch.

PYLADES
With thee I did at least; I ought also to suffer these things in common with thee.   914

ORESTES
Take thyself back to thy father, do not die with me. For thou indeed hast a city (but I no longer have), and the mansion of thy father, and a great harbor of wealth. But thou art frustrated in thy marriage with this unhappy virgin, whom I betrothed to thee, revering thy friendship. Nevertheless do thou, contracting other nuptials, be a blest father, but the connection between me and thee no longer subsists. But thou, darling name of my converse, farewell, be happy, for this is

not allowed me, but it is to thee; for we, the dead, are
deprived of happiness.   923

PYLADES
Surely thou art wide astray from my purposes. Nor may the
fruitful plain receive my blood, nor the bright air, if ever
I betraying thee, having freed myself, forsake thee; for I
committed the slaughter with thee (I will not deny it), and
I planned all things, for which now thou sufferest vengeance.
Die then I must with thee and her together, for her, whose
marriage I have courted, I consider as my wife; for what good
excuse ever shall I give, going to the Delphian land to the
citadel of the Phocians, I, who was present with you, your
friend, before indeed you were unfortunate, but now, when you
are unfortunate, am no longer thy friend? It is not possible—
but these things are my care also. But since we are about to
die, let us come to a common conference, how Menelaus may be
involved in our calamity.   936

ORESTES
O thou dearest man: for would I could see this and die!

PYLADES
Be persuaded then, but defer the slaughtering sword.

ORESTES
I will defer, if any how I can avenge myself on my enemy.

PYLADES
Be silent then, for I have but small confidence in women.

ORESTES
Do not at all fear these, for they are friends that are
present.   941

PYLADES
Let us kill Helen, which will cause great grief to
Menelaus.

ORESTES
How? for the will is here, if it can be done with glory.

PYLADES
Stabbing her; but she is lurking in thy house.   944

ORESTES
Yes indeed, and is putting her seal on all my effects.

PYLADES
But she shall seal no more, having Pluto for her bridegroom.

ORESTES
And how can this be? for she has a train of barbarian attendants.

PYLADES
Whom? for I would be afraid of no Phrygian.

ORESTES
Such men as should preside over mirrors and scents.

PYLADES
For has she brought hither her Trojan fineries?　　950

ORESTES
Oh yes! so that Greece is but a cottage for her.

PYLADES
A race of slaves is a mere nothing against a race that will not be slaves.

ORESTES
In good truth, this if I could achieve, I shrink not from two deaths.

PYLADES
But neither do I indeed, if I could revenge thee at least.

ORESTES
Disclose thy purpose, and go through it as thou sayest.

PYLADES
We will enter then the house, as men about to die.　　956

ORESTES
Thus far I comprehend, but the rest I do not comprehend.

PYLADES
We will make our lamentation to her of the things we suffer.

ORESTES
So that she shall weep, though joyed within her heart.

PYLADES
And the same things will be for us to do afterwards, which she does then.   960

ORESTES
Then how shall we finish the contest?

PYLADES
We will wear our swords concealed beneath our robes.

ORESTES
But what slaughter can there be before her attendants?

PYLADES
We will bolt them out, scattered in different parts of the house.

ORESTES
And him that is not silent we must kill.   965

PYLADES
Then the circumstances of the moment will point out what steps to take.

ORESTES
To kill Helen, I understand the sign.   967

PYLADES
Thou seest: but hear on what honorable principles I meditate it. For, if we draw our sword on a more modest woman, the murder would blot our names with infamy. But in the present instance, she shall suffer vengeance for the whole of Greece, whose fathers she slew, and made the brides bereaved of their spouses; there shall be a shout, and they will kindle up fire to the Gods, praying for many blessings to fall to thee and me, inasmuch as we shed the blood of a wicked woman. But thou shalt not be called the matricide, when thou hast slain her, but dropping this name thou shalt arrive at better things, being styled the slayer of the havoc-dealing Helen. It never, never were right that Menelaus should be prosperous, and that thy father, and thee, and thy sister should die, and thy mother; (this I forbear, for it is not decorous to mention;) and that he should seize thy house, having recovered his bride by the means of Agamemnon's valor. For may I live no longer, if I draw not my black sword upon her. But if then we do not compass the murder of Helen, having fired the palace

we will die, for we shall have glory, succeeding in one of
these two things, nobly dying, or nobly rescued.   986

CHORUS

The daughter of Tyndarus is an object of detestation to
all women, being one that has given rise to scandal against
the sex.

ORESTES

Alas! There is no better thing than a real friend, not
riches, not kingdoms; but the popular applause becomes a thing
of no account to receive in exchange for a generous friend.
For thou contrivedst the destruction that befell Aegisthus,
and wast close to me in my dangers. But now again thou givest
me to revenge me on mine enemies, and art not out of the way—
but I will leave off praising thee, since there is some burden
even in this "to be praised to excess." But I altogether in
a state of death, wish to do something to my foes and die,
that I may in turn destroy those who betrayed me, and those
may groan who also made me unhappy. I am the son of Agamemnon,
who ruled over Greece by general consent; no tyrant, but yet
he had the power as it were of a God, whom I will not disgrace,
suffering a slavish death, but breathe out my soul in freedom,
but on Menelaus will I revenge me. For if we could gain this
one thing, we should be prosperous, if from any chance safety
should come unhoped for on the slayers then, not the slain:
this I pray for. For what I wish is sweet to delight the mind
without fear of cost, though with but fleeting words uttered
through the mouth.   1007

ELECTRA

I, O brother, think that this very thing brings safety to
thee, and thy friend, and in the third place to me.

ORESTES

Thou meanest the providence of the Gods: but where is this?
for I know that there is understanding in thy mind.   1010

ELECTRA

Hear me then, and thou too give thy attention.

ORESTES

Speak, since the existing prospect of good affords some
pleasure.

ELECTRA

Art thou acquainted with the daughter of Helen?
Thou knowest her of whom I ask.

ORESTES

I know her, Hermione, whom my mother brought up.   1015

ELECTRA

She is gone to Clytemnestra's tomb.

ORESTES

For what purpose? what hope dost thou suggest?

ELECTRA

To pour libations on the tomb in behalf of her mother.

ORESTES

And what is this, thou hast told me of, that regards our
safety?

ELECTRA

Seize her as a pledge as she is coming back.   1020

ORESTES

What remedy for the three friends is this thou sayest?

ELECTRA

When Helen is dead, if Menelaus does any harm to thee or
Pylades, or me (for this firm of friendship is all one), say
that thou wilt kill Hermione; but thou oughtest to draw thy
sword, and hold it to the neck of the virgin. And if indeed
Menelaus save thee, anxious that the virgin may not die; when
he sees Helen's corse weltering in blood, give back the virgin
for her father to enjoy; but should he, not governing his
angry temper, slay thee, do thou also plunge the sword into
the virgin's neck, and I think that he, though at first he
come to us very big, will after a season soften his heart;
for neither is he brave nor valiant: this is the fortress of
our safety that I have; my arguments on the subject have been
spoken.   1033

ORESTES

O thou that hast indeed the mind of a man, but a form among
women beautiful, to what a degree art thou more worthy of
life than death! Pylades, wilt thou miserably be disappointed
of such a woman, or dwelling with her obtain this happy
marriage?   1037

PYLADES

For would it could be so! and she could come to the city of the Phocians meeting with her deserts in splendid nuptials!

ORESTES

But when will Hermione come to the house? Since for the rest thou saidst most admirably, if we could succeed in taking the whelp of the impious father.   1041

ELECTRA

Even now I guess that she must be near the house, for with this supposition the space itself of the time coincides.

ORESTES

It is well; do thou therefore, my sister Electra, waiting before the house, meet the arrival of the virgin. And watch, lest any one, either some ally, or the brother of my father, should be beforehand with us coming to the palace: and make some noise towards the house, either knocking at the doors, or sending thy voice within. But let us, O Pylades (for thou undertakest this labor with me), entering in, arm our hands with the sword to one last attempt. O my father, that inhabitest the realms of gloomy night, Orestes thy son invokes thee to come a succor to thy suppliants; for on thy account I wretched suffer unjustly, and am betrayed by thy brother, myself having acted justly: whose wife I wish to take and destroy; but be thou our accomplice in this affair.   1054

ELECTRA

O father, come then, if beneath the earth thou hearest thy children calling, who die for thee.

PYLADES

O thou relation of my father, give ear, Agamemnon, to my prayers also, preserve thy children.

ORESTES

I slew my mother.

PYLADES

But I directed the sword.

ELECTRA

But I at least incited you, and freed you from delays

ORESTES

Succoring thee, my father.   1060

ELECTRA

Neither did I forsake thee.

PYLADES

Wilt thou not therefore, hearing these things that are brought against thee , defend thy children?

ORESTES

I pour libations on thee with my tears.

ELECTRA

And I with lamentations.   1064

PYLADES

Cease, and let us haste forth to the work, for if prayers penetrate under the earth, he hears; but, Jove our ancestor, and thou revered deity of justice, grant us to succeed, him, and myself, and this virgin, for over us three friends one hazard, one cause impends, either for all to live, or all to die!   1069

ELECTRA, CHORUS

ELECTRA

O dear Mycenian virgins, who have the first place at the Pelasgian seat of the Argives;—

CHORUS

What voice art thou uttering, my respected mistress? for this appellation still awaits thee in the city of the Danaids.

ELECTRA

Arrange yourselves, some of you in this beaten way, and some there, in that other path, to guard the house.

CHORUS

But on what account dost thou command this, tell me, my friend.

ELECTRA

Fear possesses me, lest any one being in the palace, on account of this murderous deed, should contrive evils on evils.   1075

SEMICHORUS

Go, let us hasten, I indeed will guard this path, that tends towards where the sun flings his first rays.

SEMICHORUS

And I indeed this, which leads towards the west.

ELECTRA

Now turn the glances of your eyes around in every position, now here, now there, then take some other view.

CHORUS

We are, as thou commandest.

ELECTRA

Now roll your eyelids over your pupils, glance them every way through your ringlets.   1080

SEMICHORUS

Is this any one here appearing in the path?—
Who is this rustic that is standing about thy palace?

ELECTRA

We are undone then, my friends; he will immediately shew to the enemy the lurking beasts of prey armed with their swords.   1084

SEMICHORUS

Be not afraid, the path is clear, which thou thinkest not.

ELECTRA

But what?—does all with you remain secure? Give me some good report, whether the space before the hall be empty?

SEMICHORUS

All here at least is well, but look to thy province, for no one of the Danaids is approaching towards us.

SEMICHORUS

Thy report agrees with mine, for neither is there a disturbance here.   1089

ELECTRA

Come now,—I will listen at the door: why do ye delay, ye that are within, to sacrifice the victim, now that ye are in quiet?—They hear not: Alas me! wretched in misery! Are the swords then struck dumb at her beauty?

Perhaps some Argive in arms rushing in with the foot of succor will approach the palace.—Now watch more carefully; it is no contest that admits delay; but turn your eyes some this way, and some that.   1095

CHORUS
I turn each different way, looking about on all sides.

HELEN
(Within.)
Oh! Pelasgian Argos! I am miserably slain!

ELECTRA
Heard ye? The men are employing their head in the murder.— It is the shriek of Helen, as I may conjecture.

SEMICHORUS
O eternal might of Jove, come to assist my friends in every way.   1100

HELEN
Menelaus, I die! But thou art at hand, and dost not help me!

ELECTRA
Kill, strike, slay, plunging with your hands the two double-edged swords into the deserter of her father, the deserter of her husband, who destroyed numbers of the Grecians perishing by the spear at the river, whence tears fell into conjunction with tears, fell on account of the iron weapons around the whirlpools of Scamander.   1106

CHORUS
Be still, be still: I heard the sound of some one coming along the path around the palace.

ELECTRA
O most dear women, in the midst of the slaughter behold Hermione is present; let us cease from our clamor, for she comes about to fall into the meshes of our toils. A goodly prey will she be, if she be taken. Again to your stations with a calm countenance, and with a color that shall not give evidence of what has been done. I too will preserve a pensive cast of countenance, as though perfectly unacquainted with what has happened.   1115

HERMIONE, ELECTRA, CHORUS

ELECTRA

O virgin, art thou come from crowning Clytemnestra's tomb,
and pouring libations to her manes?

HERMIONE

I am come, having obtained her good services; but some
terror has come upon me, on account of the noise in the
palace, which I hear being a far distance off the house.

ELECTRA

But why? There have happened to us things worthy of groans.

HERMIONE

Speak good words; but what news dost thou tell me?   1121

ELECTRA

It has been decreed by this land, that Orestes and I die.

HERMIONE

No, I hope not so; you, who are my relations.

ELECTRA

It is fixed; but we stand under the yoke of necessity.

HERMIONE

Was the noise then in the house on this account?   1125

ELECTRA

For falling down a suppliant at the knees of Helen, he
cries out

HERMIONE

Who? for I know no more, except thou tellest me.

ELECTRA

The wretched Orestes, that he may not die, and in behalf
of me.

HERMIONE

For a just reason then the house lamented.   1129

ELECTRA

For on what other account should one rather cry out? But
come, and join in supplication with thy friends, falling clown
before thy mother, the supremely blest, that Menelaus will

not see us perish. But, O thou, that receivedst thy education at the hands of my mother, pity us, and alleviate our sufferings. Come hither to the trial; but I will lead the way, for thou alone hast the ends of our preservation.   1135

HERMIONE

Behold I direct my footstep towards the house. Be preserved, as far as lies in me.

ELECTRA

O ye in the house, my dear warriors, will ye not take your prey?

HERMIONE

Alas me! who are these I see?

ORESTES
(Advancing.)

Thou must be silent; for thou art come to preserve us, not thyself.   1140

ELECTRA

Hold her, hold her; and pointing a sword to her neck be silent, that Menelaus may know, that having found men, not Phrygian cowards, he has treated them in a manner he should treat cowards. What ho! what ho! my friends, make a noise, a noise, and shout before the palace, that the murder that is perpetrated spread not a dread alarm amongst the Argives, so that they run to assist to the king's palace, before I plainly see the slaughtered Helen lying weltering in her blood within the house, or else we hear the report from some of her attendants. For part of the havoc I know, and part not accurately.   1150

CHORUS

With justice came the vengeance of the Gods on Helen. For she filled the whole of Greece with tears on account of the ruthless, ruthless Idean Paris, who brought the Grecian state to Ilium. But be silent, for the bolts of the royal mansion resound, for some one of the Phrygians comes forth, from whom we shall hear of the affairs within the house, in what state they are.   1155

PHRYGIAN, CHORUS

PHRYGIAN

I have escaped from death by the Argive sword in these barbaric slippers, climbing over the cedar beams of the bed and the Doric triglyphs, by the flight of a barbarian. Thou art gone, thou art gone, O my country, my country! Alas me! whither can I escape, strangers, flying through the hoary air, or the sea, which the Ocean, with head in shape like a bull's, rolling with his arms encircles the earth?   1161

CHORUS

But what is the matter, attendant of Helen, thou man of Ida?

PHRYGIAN

O Ilion, Ilion! alas me! O thou fertile Phrygian city, thou sacred mount of Ida, how do I lament for thee destroyed, a sad , sad strain for my barbaric voice, on account of that form of the hapless, hapless Helen, born from a bird, the offspring of the beauteous Leda in shape of a swan, the fiend of the splendid Apollonian Pergamus! Alas! Oh! lamentations! lamentations! O wretched Dardania, warlike school of Ganymede, the companion of Jove!   1169

CHORUS

Relate to us clearly each circumstance that happened in the house, for I do not understand your former account, but merely conjecture.

PHRYGIAN

A'iXvov! A'iXivov!   1172
          {Schenk's note: *Pay close attention! / or Be alert!*}
The Barbarians begin the song of death in the language of Asia, Alas! alas! when the blood of kings has been poured on the earth by the ruthless swords of death. There came to the palace (that I may relate each circumstance) two Grecians, lions, of the one the leader of the Grecian host was said to be the father, the other the son of Strophius, a man of dark design; such was Ulysses, secretly treacherous, but faithful to his friends, bold in battle, skilled in war, cruel as the dragon. May he perish for his deep concealed design, the worker of evil! But they having advanced within her chamber, whom the archer Paris had as his wife, their eyes bathed with tears, they sat down in humble mien, one on each side of her, on the right and on the left, armed with swords. And around

her knees did they both fling their suppliant hands, around the knees of Helen did they fling them. But the Phrygian attendants sprung up, and fled in amazement: and one called out to another in terror, See, lest there be treachery. To some indeed there appeared no danger; but to others the dragon stained with his mother's blood appeared bent to enfold in his closest toils the daughter of Tyndarus.   1192

CHORUS

But where wert thou then, or hadst thou long before fled through fear?

PHRYGIAN

After the Phrygian fashion I chanced with the close circle of feathers to be fanning the gale, that sported in the ringlets of Helen, before her cheek, after the barbaric fashion.   1195

But she was winding with her fingers the flax round the distaff, but what she had spun she let fall on the ground, desirous of making from the Phrygian spoils a robe of purple as an ornament for the tomb, a gift to Clytemnestra. But Orestes entreated the Spartan girl; "O daughter of Jove, here, place thy footstep on the ground, rising from thy seat, come to the place of our ancestor Pelops, the ancient altar, that thou mayest hear my words." And he leads her, but she followed, not dreaming of what was about to happen. But his accomplice, the wicked Phocian, attended to other points. "Will ye not depart from out of the way, but are the Phrygians always vile?" and he bolted us out scattered in different parts of the house, some in the stables of the horses, and some in the out-houses, and some here and there, dispersing them some one way, some another, afar from their mistress.

CHORUS

What calamity took place after this?   1211

PHRYGIAN

O powerful, powerful Idean mother, alas! alas! the murderous sufferings, and the lawless evils, which I saw, I saw in the royal palace! From beneath their purple robes concealed having their drawn swords in their hands, they turned each his eye on either side, lest any one might chance to be present. But like mountain boars standing over against the lady, they say, "Thou shalt die, thou shalt die! thy vile husband kills thee, having given up the offspring of his brother to die at Argos." But she shrieked out, Ah me! ah me! and throwing her white arm on her breast inflicted on her head miserable blows, and, her feet turned to flight, she stepped, she stepped with her golden sandals; but Orestes thrusting his fingers into her hair, outstripping her flight, bending back her neck over his left shoulder, was about to plunge the black sword into her throat.   1225

CHORUS
Where then were the Phrygians, who dwell under the same roof, to assist her?

PHRYGIAN
With a clamor having burst by means of bars the doors and cells where we were waiting, Ave run to her assistance, each to different parts of the house, one bringing stones, another spears, another having a long-handled sword in his hand. But Pylades came against us, impetuous, like as the Phrygian Hector or Ajax in his triple-crested helmet, whom I saw, I saw at the gates of Priam: but we clashed together the points of our swords: then indeed, then did the Phrygians give clear proof how inferior we were in the force of Mars to the spear of Greece. One indeed turning away, a fugitive, but another wounded, and another deprecating the death that threatened him: but under favor of the darkness we fled: and the corses fell, but some staggered, and some lay prostrate. But the wretched Hermione came to the house at the time when her murdered mother fell to the ground, that unhappy woman that gave her birth. And running upon her as Bacchanals without their thyrsus, as a heifer in the mountains they bore her away in their hands, and again eagerly rushed upon the daughter of Jove to slay her. But she vanished altogether from the chamber through the palace. O Jupiter and earth, and light, and darkness! or by her enchantments, or by the art of magic, or by the stealth of the Gods. But of what followed I know no farther, for I sped in stealth my foot from the palace. But Menelaus having endured many, many severe toils, has received back from Troy the violated rites of Helen to no purpose.   1251

CHORUS
And see something strange succeeds to these strange things, for I see Orestes with his sword drawn walking before the palace with agitated step.

ORESTES, PHRYGIAN, CHORUS

ORESTES
Where is he that fled from my sword out of the palace?

PHRYGIAN
I supplicate thee, king, falling prostrate before thee after the barbaric fashion. 1254

ORESTES
The case before us is not in Ilium, but the Argive land.

PHRYGIAN
In every region to live is sweeter than to die, in the opinion of the wise.

ORESTES
Didst thou not raise a cry for Menelaus to come with succor?

PHRYGIAN
I indeed am present on purpose to assist thee; for thou art the more worthy.

ORESTES
Perished then the daughter of Tyndarus justly?

PHRYGIAN
Most justly, even had she three lives for vengeance.

ORESTES
With thy tongue dost thou flatter, not having these sentiments within? 1261

PHRYGIAN
For ought she not? She who utterly destroyed Greece as well as the Phrygians themselves?

ORESTES
Swear, I will kill thee else, that thou art not speaking to curry favor with me.

PHRYGIAN
By my life have I sworn, which I should wish to hold a sacred oath.

ORESTES
Was the steel thus dreadful to all the Phrygians at Troy also? 1265

PHRYGIAN
Remove thy sword, for being so near me it gleams horrid slaughter.

ORESTES

Art thou afraid, lest thou shouldest become a rock, as
though looking on the Gorgon?

PHRYGIAN

Lest I should become a corse, but I know not of the Gorgon's
head.

ORESTES

Slave as thou art, dost thou fear death, which will rid
thee from thy woes?

PHRYGIAN

Every one, although a man be a slave, rejoices to behold
the light.   1270

ORESTES

Thou sayest well; thy understanding saves thee, but go into
the house.

PHRYGIAN

Thou wilt not kill me then?

ORESTES

Thou art pardoned.

PHRYGIAN

This is good word thou hast spoken.

ORESTES

Yet we may change our measures.   1275

PHRYGIAN

But this thou sayest not well.

ORESTES

Thou art a fool, if thou thinkest I could endure to defile
me by smiting thy neck, for neither art thou a woman, nor
oughtest thou to be ranked among men. But that thou mightest
not raise a clamor came I forth out of the house: for Argos,
when it has heard a noise, is soon roused, but we have no
dread in meeting Menelaus, as far as swords go; but let him
come exulting with his golden ringlets flowing over his
shoulders, for if he collects the Argives, and brings them
against the palace seeking revenge for the death of Helen,
and is not willing to let me be in safety, and my sister, and

Pylades my accomplice in this affair, he shall see two corses,
both the virgin and his wife.   1287

CHORUS

Alas! alas! O fate, the house of the Atridae again falls
into another, another fearful struggle.

SEMICHORUS

What shall we do? shall we carry these tidings to the city,
or shall we keep in silence?

SEMICHORUS

This is the safer plan, my friends.   1290

SEMICHORUS

Behold before the house, behold this smoke leaping aloft
in the air portends *something*.

SEMICHORUS

They are lighting the torches, as about to burn down the
mansion of Tantalus, nor do they forbear from murder.

CHORUS

The God rules the events that .happen to mortals,
whichsoever way he wills. But some vast power by the
instigation of the Furies has struck, has struck these palaces
to the shedding of blood on account of the fall of Myrtilus
from the chariot.   1296
But lo! I s.ee Menelaus also here approaching the house
with a quick step, having by some means or other perceived
the calamity which now is present. Will ye not anticipate him
by closing the gates with bolts, O ye children of Atreus, who
are in the palace? A man in prosperity is a terrible thing to
those in adversity, as now thou art in misery, Orestes.

MENELAUS below, ORESTES, PYLADES, ELECTRA,
HERMIONE above, CHORUS

MENELAUS

I am present, having heard the horrid and atrocious deeds
of the two lions, for I call them not men. For I have now
heard of my wife, that she died not, but vanished away, this
that I heard was empty report, which one deceived by fright
related; but these are the artifices of the matricide, and
much derision. Open some one the door, my attendants I command
to burst open these gates here, that my child at least we may

deliver from the hand of these blood-polluted men, and may receive my unhappy, my miserable lady, with whom those murderers of my wife must die by my hand.   1311

ORESTES

What ho there! Touch not these gates with thine hands: to Menelaus I speak, that thou towerest in thy boldness, or with this pinnacle will I crush thy head, having rent down the ancient battlement, the labor of the builders. But the gates are made fast with bolts, which will hinder thee from thy purpose of bringing aid, so that thou canst not pass within the palace.   1317

MENELAUS

Ha! what is this? I see the blaze of torches, and these stationed on the battlements, on the height of the palace, and the sword placed over the neck of my daughter to guard her.   1320

ORESTES

Whether is it thy will to question, or to hear me?

MENELAUS

I wish neither, but it is necessary, as it seems, to hear thee.

ORESTES

I am about to slay thy daughter if thou wish to know.

MENELAUS

Having slain Helen, dost thou perpetrate murder on murder?

ORESTES

For would I had gained my purpose not being deluded, as I was, by the Gods.   1325

MENELAUS

Thou hast slain her, and deniest it, and speakest these things to insult me.

ORESTES

It is a denial that gives me pain, for would that—

MENELAUS

Thou had done what deed? for thou callest forth alarm.

ORESTES
I had hurled to hell the fury of Greece.

MENELAUS
Give back the body of my wife, that I may bury her in a tomb.   1330

ORESTES
Ask her of the Gods; but I will slay thy daughter.

MENELAUS
The matricide contrives murder on murder.

ORESTES
The avenger- of his father, whom thou gavest up to die.

MENELAUS
Was not the blood of thy mother formerly shed sufficient for thee?

ORESTES
I should not be weary of slaying wicked women, were I to slay them for ever.   1335

MENELAUS
Art thou also, Pylades, a partaker in this murder?

ORESTES
By his silence he assents, but if I speak, it will be sufficient.

MENELAUS
But not with impunity, unless indeed thou fliest on wings.

ORESTES
We will not fly, but will set fire to the palace?

MENELAUS
What! wilt thou destroy thy father's mansion?   1340

ORESTES
Yes, that thou mayest not possess it, will I, having stabbed this virgin here over the flames.

MENELAUS
Slay her; since having slain thou shalt at least give me satisfaction for these deeds.

                    ORESTES
It shall be so then.

                    MENELAUS
Alas! on no account do this!

                    ORESTES
Be silent then; but bear to suffer evil justly.   1345

                    MENELAUS
What! is it just for thee to live?

                    ORESTES
Yes, and to rule over the land.

                    MENELAUS
What land?

                    ORESTES
Here, in Pelasgian Argos.

                    MENELAUS
Well wouldst thou touch the sacred lavers!   1350

                    ORESTES
And pray why not?

                    MENELAUS
And wouldst slaughter the victim before the battle!

                    ORESTES
And thou wouldst most righteously.

                    MENELAUS
Yes, for I am pure as to my hands.

                    ORESTES
But not thy heart.   1355

                    MENELAUS
Who would speak to thee?

                    ORESTES
Whoever loves his father.

                    MENELAUS
And whoever reveres his mother.

                    ORESTES
—Is happy.

                    MENELAUS
Not thou at least.   1360

                    ORESTES
For wicked women please me not.

                    MENELAUS
Take away the sword from my daughter.

                    ORESTES
Thou art false in thy expectations.

                    MENELAUS
But wilt thou kill my daughter?

                    ORESTES
Thou art no longer false.   1365

                    MENELAUS
Alas me! what shall I do?

                    ORESTES
Go to the Argives, and persuade them.

                    MENELAUS
With what persuasion?

                    ORESTES
Beseech the city that we may not die.

                    MENELAUS
Otherwise ye will slay my daughter?   1370

                    ORESTES
The thing is so.

                    MENELAUS
O wretched Helen!—

                    ORESTES
And am I not wretched?

                    MENELAUS
I brought thee hither from the Trojans to be a victim.

ORESTES

For would this were so!   1375

MENELAUS

Having endured ten thousand toils.

ORESTES

Except on my account.

MENELAUS

I have met with dreadful treatment.

ORESTES

For then, when thou oughtest, thou wert of no assistance.

MENELAUS

Thou hast me.   1380

ORESTES

Thou at least hast caught thyself. But, ho there! set fire to the palace, Electra, from beneath; and thou, Pylades, the most true of my friends, light up these battlements of the walls.

MENELAUS

O land of the Danai, and inhabitants of warlike Argos, will ye not, ho there! come in arms to my succor? For this man here, having perpetrated the shocking murder of his mother, brings destruction on your whole city, that he may live.

APOLLO

Menelaus, cease from thy irritated state of mind; I Phoebus the son of Latona, in thy presence, am addressing thee. Thou too, Orestes, who standest over that damsel with thy sword drawn, that thou mayest know what commands I bring with me. Helen indeed, whom thou minded to destroy, working Menelaus to anger, didst fail of thy purpose, she is here, whom ye see wrapt in the bosom of the sky, preserved, and not slain by thy hands. Her I preserved, and snatched from thy sword, commanded by my father Jove. For being the daughter of Jove, it is right that she should live immortal.   1395

And she shall have her seat by Castor and Pollux in the bosom of the sky, the guardian of mariners. But take to thyself another bride, and lead her home, since for the beauty of this woman the Gods brought together the Greeks and Trojans, and caused deaths, that they might draw from oft' the earth the pride of mortals, who had become an infinite multitude. Thus is it with regard to Helen but thee, on the other hand, Orestes, it behooveth, having passed beyond the boundaries of this land, to inhabit the Parrhasian plain during the revolution of a year, and it shall be called by a name after thy flight, so that the Azanes and Arcadians shall call it Oresteum: and thence having departed to the city of the Athenians, undergo the charge of shedding thy mother's blood laid by the three Furies. But the Gods the arbiters of the cause shall pass on thee most sacredly their decree on the hill of Mars, in which it behooveth thee to be victorious. But Hermione, to whose neck thou art holding the sword, it is destined for thee, Orestes, to wed, but Neoptolemus, who thinks to marry her, shall never marry her. For it is fated to him to die by the Delphic sword, as he is demanding of me satisfaction for his father Achilles. But to Pylades give thy sister's hand, as thou didst formerly agree, but a happy life now coming on awaits him. But, O Menelaus, suffer Orestes to reign over Argos. But depart and rule over the Spartan land, having it as thy wife's dowry, who exposing thee to numberless evils always was bringing thee to this. But what regards the city I will make all right for him, I, who compelled him to slay his mother.   1422

ORESTES

O Loxian prophet, thou wert not then a false prophet in thine oracles, but a true one. And yet a fear comes upon me, that having heard one of the Furies, I might think that I have been hearing thy voice. But it is well fulfilled, and I will obey thy words. Behold I let go Hermione from slaughter, and approve her alliance, whenever her father shall give her.

MENELAUS

O Helen, daughter of Jove, hail! but I bless thee inhabiting the happy mansions of the Gods. But to thee, Orestes, do I betroth my daughter at Phoebus' commands, but illustrious thyself marrying from an illustrious family, be happy, both thou and I who give her.   1432

APOLLO

Now depart each of you whither we have appointed, and dissolve your quarrels.

MENELAUS

It is our duty to obey.

ORESTES

I too entertain the same sentiments, and I receive with
friendship thee in thy sufferings, O Menelaus, and thy
oracles, O Apollo.   1436

APOLLO

Go now, each his own way, honoring the most excellent
goddess Peace; but I will convey Helen to the mansions of
Jove, passing through the pole of the shining stars, where
sitting by Juno, and Hercules' Hebe, a goddess, she shall
ever be honored by mortals with libations, in conjunction
with the Tyndaridae, the sons of Jove, presiding over the sea
to the benefit of mariners.

CHORUS

O greatly glorious Victory, mayest thou uphold my life,
and cease not from crowning me!   1444

(Exit.)

(LIGHTS FADE.)

(CURTAINS.)

(END OF PLAY.)

HELEN

HELEN

PERSONS REPRESENTED

HELEN

TEUCER

CHORUS

MENELAUS

OLD WOMAN

MESSENGER

THEONOE

THEOCLYMENUS

MESSENGER EXTRAORDINARY

CASTOR and POLLUX

THE ARGUMENT

Herodotus states that Helen never was at Troy at all, but that a phantom was sent in her stead, she herself being carried into Egypt. Upon this tradition Euripides has constructed the following play.

As long as Proteus was king of Egypt, Helen remained unmolested, but upon his death his son Theoclymenus tried to obtain her in marriage. In despair she took refuge at the tomb of Proteus, where she met with Menelaus, who had been shipwrecked on the coast. A recognition took place, and by the aid of Theonoe, they effected their escape under a pretense of paying funeral rites to the drowned Menelaus. Upon discovering how he had been deceived, Theoclymenus, enraged with his sister Theonoe for not acquainting him with the fact that Menelaus was really alive and present, would have slain her; but was prevented by the intervention of the Dioscuri.

HELEN

These indeed are the fair virgin-streams of the Nile, which, in the place of heaven-sent showers, waters the plain of Egypt, when the white snow melts (over) the fields. But Proteus, whilst he lived, was the ruler of this land, inhabiting the island Pharos, but the king of Egypt; who marries Psamathe, one of the virgins of the sea, when she had left the bed of Aeacus. And she bears two children to this house, Theoclymenus, a male, (so called) because forsooth he passed his life reverencing the Gods, and a virgin noble in form, the pride of her mother while she was an infant, but when she arrived at an age ripe for nuptials, they call her Theonoe; for she knew all things divine, both things that are and shall be, receiving the gift from her ancestor Nereus. But to me indeed there is a country-land, not unrenowned, Sparta, and my father is Tyndarus. And there is a certain story that Jove flew down upon my mother, assuming the form of a swan; that, pretending to flee from an eagle's pursuit, accomplished stealthy nuptials, if this story be true. And I was called Helen; and I will narrate the evils which I have suffered. [19]

There came (to a contest) of beauty in the Idaean recess, before Alexander, three Goddesses, Juno, and Venus, and the Jove-born virgin, wishing to undergo his judgment of their form. Now Venus, holding forth my beauty, (if misfortune is beautiful,) so that Alexander may marry it, prevails; and the Idaean Paris, quitting his cattle-stalls, came to Sparta, as about to possess my bed. But Juno, indignant that she does not surpass the Goddesses, gave my nuptials with Alexander to the winds; and gives to the son of king Priam not me, but a breathing image formed of ether, making it like myself. [28]

And he thinks (vain thought!) that he has me, not having me. And other devices of Jove go along with these evils. For he brought war upon the land of the Greeks, and on the wretched Phrygians, that he might lighten mother earth of a crowd and multitude of mortals, and might make known the mightiest in Greece. And I was placed in the power of the Phrygians, not myself indeed, but my name, as a prize of the spear for the Greeks. And Hermes, taking me up in folds of ether, having hidden me in a cloud, (for Jove did not neglect me,) settled me in this house of Proteus, having chosen out the most temperate of all mortals, in order that I might preserve the bed of Menelaus undefiled. And I indeed am here; but my wretched husband, having assembled an army, is hunting out my ravishers, setting out to the fortresses of Troy. And through me many souls have perished at Scamander's stream, and I, the sufferer of all, am accursed, and seem, having deserted my own husband, to have lit up a great war against the Greeks. Why then do I yet live? I have heard this saying from the God Hermes, that I shall yet dwell in the renowned land of Sparta with my husband, he having learned that I did not come to Troy, so that I could not spread my couch for any (other).   49

As long, therefore, as Proteus beheld this light of the sun, I was held sacred from nuptials; but when he was hidden in the gloom of the earth, the son of the deceased hunts me down to marry me. But respecting my husband of old, I have fallen a suppliant at this monument of Proteus, that it may preserve my bed for my husband; so that, if throughout Greece I bear a name of ill repute, my body at least may not pay the debt of shame here.   56

TEUCHER

Who has the rule over these fortified dwellings? For the house is fit to be guessed as one of wealth, since both the porticoes are regal, and the mansion well turreted. Ha, ye Gods, what sight have I seen? I behold that most hated, murderous image of a woman, who has undone me, and all the Greeks. The Gods abhor thee, in as fur as thou hast the likeness of Helen! But if I had not held my foot in a strange land, with this stone well-aimed thou shouldst have died, as the consequence of thy likeness to the daughter of Jove.   64

HELEN

Why, O wretched man, dost thou, whoever thou art, loathe me, and hate me for her misfortunes?

TEUCHER

I was wrong, and yielded more to wrath than became me; for all Greece hates the daughter of Jove. But excuse me for my words, O lady.   67

HELEN

But who art thou? from whence hast thou turned thyself to the plains of this earth?

TEUCHER

One of the unhappy Greeks, O lady.   70

HELEN

It is not then to be wondered if you hate Helen. But who art thou, of whom (born)? It behooves thee to speak.

TEUCHER
My name is Teucer; and the father, who begat me, is Telamon;
and Salamis is the country that nurtured me.

HELEN
Why then dost thou visit these fields of the Nile?

TEUCHER
I have been driven an exile out of my father-land.   75

HELEN
Thou must be unhappy. And who casts thee out of thy country?

TEUCHER
Telamon, my father. Whom could you have more friendly?

HELEN
Through what? for the matter carries with it some calamity.

TEUCHER
My brother Ajax, dying in Troy, was my ruin.

HELEN
How? not, surely, deprived of life by thy sword?   80

TEUCHER
A leap upon his own sword destroyed him.

HELEN
Being mad? For who in his senses would dare this thing?

TEUCHER
Knowest thou a certain Achilles, the son of Peleus?

HELEN
He once on a time came a suitor for Helen, as we hear.

TEUCHER
He dying, caused among his allies a strife for his arms.

HELEN
And what ill then does this become to Ajax?   86

TEUCHER
Through another receiving the arms, he removed himself from
life.

                         HELEN
Then thou art sickening at his woes?

                        TEUCHER
Ay, because I did not perish together with him.

                         HELEN
And didst thou arrive, O stranger, at the renowned city of
Troy?   90

                        TEUCHER
Ay, and having destroyed it, myself was destroyed in turn.

                         HELEN
For is it already burnt and consumed with fire?

                        TEUCHER
Ay, so that there is not a clear vestige of the walls.

                         HELEN
O miserable Helen, through thee the Phrygians have
perished.   94

                        TEUCHER
Ay, and the Greeks besides; and great evils have been done.

                         HELEN
How long a time has the city been destroyed?

                        TEUCHER
About seven fruit-bearing circles of years.

                         HELEN
And how long was the other time you remained in Troy?

                        TEUCHER
Many moons, passing through ten years.

                         HELEN
And did you take the Spartan woman?   100

                        TEUCHER
Menelaus led her away, seizing her by the hair.

                         HELEN
Didst thou behold the unhappy woman? Or dost thou speak
from hearsay?

TEUCHER
Ay, as I see thee with my eyes, nothing less.

HELEN
Consider lest ye had a vision sent by the Gods.

TEUCHER
Speak of some other subject, no longer of her.   105

HELEN
Are ye thus certain in your opinion?

TEUCHER
(Yes,) for I saw her myself with mine eyes, and my mind
sees her.

HELEN
And is Menelaus now in his dwelling with his wife?

TEUCHER
He is not yet in Argos, nor at the streams of Eurotas.

HELEN
Alas! thou hast told this ill to those to whom thou art
speaking.   110

TEUCHER
It is rumored that he is vanished with his wife.

HELEN
Was there not the same voyage for all the Greeks?

TEUCHER
There was; but a tempest drove each different ways.

HELEN
On what surface of the ocean main?

TEUCHER
As they passed the midway waves of the Aegean road.   115

HELEN
And from this time does no one know of Menelaus' arrival?

TEUCHER
Not one; but it is rumored through Greece that he is dead.

HELEN
We are undone. But is the daughter of Thestias alive?

TEUCHER
Dost thou mean Leda? She indeed is gone dead.   119

HELEN
What, did the disgraceful reputation of Helen destroy her?

TEUCHER
They say so, having fitted her noble neck to the noose.

HELEN
But are the sons of Tyndarus alive, or not alive?

TEUCHER
They are dead, and are not dead; for there are two stories.

HELEN
Which is the better one? O wretched I on account of my troubles!

TEUCHER
They say that they two, likened to stars, are Gods.   125

HELEN
Well hast thou spoken this. But what is the other (report)?

TEUCHER
That by suicide on their sister's account they breathed out life. But enough of discourse, I do not desire to grieve twice. But, in the matter on account of which I came to this regal house, desiring to see the prophetic Theonoe, do thou aid a stranger, that I may obtain oracular responses, how I may steer my ship's sail prosperously to the sea-coast land of Cyprus, where Apollo foretold that I should dwell, giving it the island name of Salamis, for the sake of my former country.   134

HELEN
The voyage itself will show, O stranger; but do thou, quitting this land, fly, before the son of Proteus, who rules this land, sees thee. For he is absent, trusting to his hounds, in beast-slaying huntings. For he murders whatever Grecian stranger he takes. But for what reason, do not thou seek to learn, and I keep silence. For what should I avail thee?   140

TEUCHER

Well hast thou spoken, O lady; and may the Gods give thee a reward for thy good counsel. But thou, possessing a form like Helen's, has not a like disposition, but very different. But ill may she perish, nor come to the streams of Eurotas; but mayest thou be ever fortunate, lady.   144

HELEN

O thou that art beginning a mighty piteous strain of woes, what groan shall I vie in uttering? Or what song shall I commence, with tears, with lamentations, or mourning? Woe! woe! ye Sirens, winged youthful virgins, daughters of Earth, would that ye might come to (join with) my groans, having the Libyan pipe, or the syrinx; tears connected with my lamentable woes, sufferings with sufferings, and dirges with dirges; and may Proserpine send companies of singers in harmony with dirges, deadly, deadly, that by tears she may receive from me the favor of the dead who have perished, beneath her gloomy dwelling.   154

CHORUS

Around the blue-surfaced ocean I chanced to be warming in the sun's golden rays my purple garments, on the tufted herbage, and on the fresh-sprung reeds, whence (I heard the plaintive, unmusical elegy) some nymph uttered a piteous cry, lamenting with mournings whatever it was she shrieked forth, like a Naiad on the mountains, uttering a wandering sad strain, and beneath the rocky dells she bemoans the ravishment of Pan.   161

HELEN

Alas! alas! ye Grecian girls, prey of the barbarian ship, a sailor of the Greeks has come, ah! has come, bearing to me tears upon tears, the destruction of Troy, a care for the hostile flame, through me the many-slayer, through my name of many troubles. And Leda in the noose has received her death through grief for my shame. And my much-wandering husband perishing at sea is no more, and the twin-born glory of their country, Castor and his brother, have left, vanishing, vanishing, the horse-trodden plains, and the gymnasia of reedy Eurotas, a fit toil for youths.   170

CHORUS

Alas! alas! O, for thy fortune of much grief, and thy fate, lady. A life not to be lived has been thy lot, has been thy lot, when by thy mother Jove begot thee, conspicuous in the sky, with the snow-colored plumage of a swan. For what of ills is wanting to thee? And what life hast thou not endured? Thy mother indeed is no more, and the twin beloved sons of Jove are not faring prosperously; and thou beholdest not thy country-land, and through the city goes a report, that bestows thee, honored lady, on a barbarian bed. But thy (husband) has quitted life amid the waves of the sea, nor wilt thou ever again bless thy father's house and the Goddess of the brazen house.   181

HELEN

Alas! alas! who was it of the Phrygians, or who from the Grecian land, that cut down the pine causing tears to Troy? Whence having fitted together the destructive bark, the son of Priam sailed in a barbarian ship to my hearth, after my ill-fated beauty, that he might obtain me in marriage. And the crafty, many-slaying Venus, bringing death upon the sons of Danaus and Priam, (sent him). O wretched for my calamity! But she who sits on golden thrones, Juno, the dignified spouse of Jove, sent the swift-footed son of Maia, who carried me off through the air, while gathering fresh rosebuds in my robe, that I might visit Minerva of the brazen temple, and has placed me unhappy in this land, for an unhappy strife, a strife to the sons of Priam with Greece. And my name has, near the streams of Simois, an ill report in vain.   194

CHORUS

Thou hast, I know, grievous sufferings; but it is expedient for thee to bear the necessary events of life as easily as possible.

HELEN

Ye dear women, to what a fate have I been yoked! Did not my mother bring me forth as a prodigy to men? For neither Greek nor barbarian woman has given birth to a white vessel of younglings, in which they say Leda begot me by Jove. For my life and affairs are a prodigy; in part through Juno; but of some my beauty is the cause. Would that, being sponged out, like a picture, I might again in turn receive a foul appearance instead of a fair one; and would that the evil chances, which I now endure, the Greeks had forgotten, but preserved the good (in memory) as they preserve my bad. Whosoever therefore, looking to one fate only, is ill-treated by the Gods, it is a thing heavy indeed, but may nevertheless be borne; but I lie amidst many calamities. First indeed, not being unjust, I am in ill repute; and this is a greater evil than the truth, when any one is charged with evils he does not possess. Then the Gods have removed me from my country-land to barbarian customs; and bereft of friends, I have become a slave, born of free parents; for amongst barbarians all are slaves, save one. But one anchor alone has supported my fortunes, that my husband would some time come, and release me from ills. He is dead, he is now no more. And my mother is dead; and I am her murderess, unjustly indeed; yet is that injustice mine. And my daughter, who was the ornament of mine house and self, grows grey in unwedded virginity; and the Dioscuri, the reputed twin sons of Jove, exist no more.   220

But having all things unfortunate, I am dead in circumstances, but not in deed. And what is the last of all— if I were to arrive at my country, I should be confined by bars, persons thinking that (the real) Helen had come, who had been at Troy with Menelaus. For if my husband were alive, I should be recognized, proceeding to the proofs by tokens, which would be evident to us alone. But now there neither is this (hope), nor will he be ever saved. Why then do I longer live? In what misfortune am I deficient? Shall I, choosing nuptials as a release from ills, live with a barbarian husband, sitting at a wealthy table? But when a husband is bitter to a stranger woman, even to be saved is bitter. 'Tis best to die? How then shall I die honorably? Unseemly indeed are hangings aloft, and even among slaves it is thought unbecoming; but cutting the throat has something noble and glorious, and of little account is the time to free oneself from life. For into such a depth of woes have we come; since other women are fortunate indeed through their beauty, but me has this very thing undone.   238

CHORUS
Do not, Helen, think that the stranger, whoever he be who has arrived, has told all things truly.

HELEN
And yet he stated clearly that my husband had perished.

CHORUS
Many words may be spoken even to a false purport.

HELEN
Ay, and, on the contrary, clear ones to a true.

CHORUS
For thou art carried to calamity rather than to good.

HELEN
For a fear, surrounding me, leads me to apprehension.

CHORUS
But how hast thou a kind reception in this house?   245

HELEN
All are my friends save he who seeks my nuptials.

CHORUS
Do then, knowest thou what? Quitting the seat of the
monument—

HELEN
To what discourse or advice art thou slowly coming?   248

CHORUS
Going into the house, inquire of Theonoe, who knows every
thing, as the virgin is descended from the marine daughter of
Nereus, concerning thy husband, whether he is yet alive, or
has quitted the light; and having well ascertained the fact,
regulate your joy and lamentation according to your fortunes.
But before thou knowest aught rightly, what will it profit
thee to be in sorrow? But be persuaded by me; quitting this
tomb, mix in company with the virgin, from whom thou wilt
know all. When thou hast in these dwellings the power of
learning the truth, why dost thou look farther? And I too
wish to enter the house with thee, and with thee to learn the
prophecies of the virgin, for it is meet that a woman should
with a woman labor.   260

HELEN
Friends, I receive your advice. Go, go into the house, that
thou mayest learn my troubles within the house.

CHORUS
Thou callest one not slowly willing.

HELEN
Alas! unhappy day, what tearful story shall I unhappy hear?

CHORUS
Do not, O dear one, anticipate lamentations like a
prophetess of woes.   265

HELEN
What has my wretched husband endured? Does he behold the
light and the four-horse chariot of the sun, and (look) up to
the tracks of the stars? or does he possess the lot of earth
among the dead below the earth?   268

CHORUS

Set down the future, whatsoever it shall be, to the better side.

HELEN

For I have called upon thee, I have sworn by thee, the damp Eurotas, green with reeds, that if this report concerning my husband's death be true—

CHORUS

What unintelligible words are these?   272

HELEN

I should wish for the deadly hanging for my neck; or, I would cause to approach the sword-slaying violence of a throat-cutting slaughter, in a contest of the very steel driven within (and) through my flesh; a sacrifice to the triple yoke of Goddesses, and to the son of Priam who cultivated the pipe in Ida near his cattle stalls.   276

CHORUS

Elsewhere may these ills be averted; but may thy state be fortunate.

HELEN

Alas! wretched Troy, thou art perishing through deeds not done, and wretched things hast thou undergone. But in the gift Venus has produced much blood and many tears, and griefs on griefs, tears on tears, f- sufferings she received. And mothers have lost their children, and virgins related to the dead have shorn their tresses around the Phrygian wave of Scamander. And Greece has shouted forth and uttered a cry, a cry, and has placed her hands on her head, and with her nails has wetted her soft-skinned chin, and with bloody blows. O thou virgin, once happy in Arcadia, Callisto, who with four-footed limbs didst once approach the bed of Jove, how much more hast thou obtained than my mother; who in the form of a hairy-limbed beast changed the griefs of thy sorrow, in the form of lioness with savage eye. And she too (more), whom once on a time Diana cast out of her chorus, the stag with golden horns, the Titanian daughter of Merops, on account of her beauty. But my person has destroyed, has destroyed the towers of Troy, and the Greeks who perished.   294

MENELAUS

O Pelops, who at Pisa didst once successfully contend with Oenomaus in the contest of cars with four steeds, would that,

when thou, being sawn asunder, didst furnish a banquet for
the Gods, thou hadst quitted life among the Gods, before thou
hadst ever begotten my father Atreus; who, by his union with
Aerope begat Agamemnon and myself, Menelaus, a renowned pair.
For I think (and this I speak not in boast) that I directed
the largest armament sent by oars against Troy, leading as a
king the expedition, not by force, but ruling over the willing
youths of Greece. And one can number up some who are now no
more, and some who, joyfully escaping from the sea, are
bearing the names of the dead home to their dwellings. But
wretched I am wandering on the marine wave of the dark-blue
sea through all the time (since) I sacked the towers of Troy;
and, seeking to go to my country, I am not granted by the
Gods to obtain this.   309

But I have sailed to the deserted and inhospitable retreats
of Libya; and when I am near my country, again the breeze
drives me back, and never does a favorable wind come upon ray
sail, so that I may reach my country. And now, a miserable
shipwrecked mariner, I have, after losing my friends, fallen
out upon this land; but my vessel is broken against the rocks
into a great number of wrecks. And the lowest plank was
(alone) left of the varied joinings, upon which I was with
difficulty saved, through an unexpected fortune, and Helen
too, whom I have dragged away from Troy. I know not however
the name of this country and the people; for I was ashamed to
fall in with the crowd, so that they should inquire about
these my squalid garments, and I conceal through shame my
misfortunes. For when a man (once) in a lofty station fares
ill, he is wont to fall into an unusual state worse than he
who has been unhappy of old. But necessity wears me down; for
neither is food at hand, nor garments round my body; but this
may be conjectured,' (seeing) I am girt round in the thrown-
out sheets of the ship. But my former robes, and splendid
coverings, and luxurious vestments, the sea has snatched
away.   329

But having hidden in the recesses of a cave the woman who
is the cause of all my troubles, I am come (hither), having
compelled my surviving friends to guard my wife. And I am
travelling alone, seeking what is advantageous for my friends
there, if perchance I can by a discovery lay hold of it. But
perceiving this dwelling, surrounded with battlements, and
the majestic portals of some wealthy man, I have approached.
And there is a hope that sailors may receive something at
least from a wealthy house; but of those who have not the
means of life, none, even if they wished, could have the power
to assist. Ho! what porter will come from the house, who will
tell my troubles (to those) within?   340

OLD WOMAN

Who is at the gates? Wilt thou not betake thyself from the house? nor, by standing at the gates of the vestibule, give trouble to the masters? Or wilt thou die, being a Greek by birth, for whom there is no regard?   343

MENELAUS

O aged dame, well dost thou speak all these words. May I— for I will obey—but defer your speech.

OLD WOMAN

Away! for this duty is laid on me, stranger, that no Greek approach this dwelling.

MENELAUS

Hold; do not stretch forth thine hand, nor drive me away by force.

OLD WOMAN

For thou art persuaded of naught that I say. Thou art the cause.

MENELAUS

Tell it to thy masters within.

OLD WOMAN

To thy cost, I think, I should tell thy words.   350

MENELAUS

I am come, a shipwrecked stranger, a race to be not without an asylum.

OLD WOMAN

Go, then, to some other house instead of this,

MENELAUS

Not so; but I will pass by within; and do thou be persuaded by me.

OLD WOMAN

Know that thou art troublesome, and thou wilt soon be pushed away by force.

MENELAUS

Alas! where are my renowned armaments?   355

                    OLD WOMAN
There, perhaps, thou wast a man to be worshipped, not so
here.

                    MENELAUS
O fortune, how unworthily have I been dishonored!

                    OLD WOMAN
Why dost thou bedew thine eyelids with tears? Wherefore
art thou in grief?

                    MENELAUS
In reference to my former happy fortunes.   360

                    OLD WOMAN
Wilt thou not, then, going away, give thy tears to thy
friends.

                    MENELAUS
But what country is this? And of whom are these the regal
abodes?

                    OLD WOMAN
Proteus inhabits these dwellings, but the land is Egypt.

                    MENELAUS
Egypt? O wretched me! whither indeed have I sailed?

                    OLD WOMAN
Why is the race of the Nile to be blamed by thee?   365

                    MENELAUS
I find no fault with it. I mourn my fate.

                    OLD WOMAN
Many fare ill, not thou, forsooth, alone.

                    MENELAUS
Is the king you name in the house?

                    OLD WOMAN
This is his monument; but his son rules the land.

                    MENELAUS
Where then is he? Is he from home or in the house?   370

OLD WOMAN
He is not within; but he is most hostile to the Greeks.

MENELAUS
Having what cause, from which I suffer?

OLD WOMAN
Helen, the daughter of Jove, is in this house.

MENELAUS
How sayest thou? What tale hast thou told? Tell it me again.

OLD WOMAN
The daughter of Tyndarus, who was once at Sparta.   375

MENELAUS
(Aside.)
Coming from whence? What meaning has this affair?

OLD WOMAN
Journeying hither from the Lacedaemonian land.

MENELAUS
(Aside.)
When? Surely I have not been robbed of my wife out of the cave.

OLD WOMAN
Before that the Greeks came to Troy, O stranger. But go from the house, for there is in the dwelling a calamity, by which the royal house is disturbed. And thou hast come at no opportune time; for if my master catch thee, death will be thy guest. For I am well inclined to the Greeks, not so (bitter to them) as the bitter words I have uttered, fearing my master.   384

MENELAUS
What shall I speak? what shall I say? for I hear of present calamities following the past; if I indeed have come, bringing my wife, who was taken captive, from Troy, and she is preserved in the cave; but some other woman, having the same name as my wife, dwells in this house. She (the old woman) said indeed that she (Helen) was born the daughter of Jove. But perhaps there is some man by the banks of Nile, possessing the name of Jove? For in heaven there is but one. But where on the earth is Sparta, save only where are the streams of

Eurotas with beautiful reeds? And the name of Tyndarus is applied to him alone. But what land bears the name of Lacedaemon, and what of Troy? I indeed have naught to say. For many persons, it seems, in the wide earth possess the same names, and city the same with city, and woman with woman. There is nothing then to be wondered at; nor, again, will I fly from the fear held forth by that woman. For there is no man so barbarous in disposition as that, having heard my name, he will not bestow food. Renowned is the flame of Troy, and I, Menelaus, who kindled it, am not unknown in the whole earth. I will wait for the ruler of the house; and (this resolution) has for me a two-fold protection. If indeed he be a cruel wretch, I will, having concealed myself, go (back) to the wreck; but if he yields to any softness, I will crave the things conducive to my present misfortunes. But being a king oneself, it is the extreme of evils for us wretched to beg of other kings for sustenance; but it needs must be. For it is not my saying, but the saying of wise men: Naught has a greater power than terrible necessity.　　411

CHORUS

I heard the prophetic maiden, who appeared and gave out the oracles to the royal household, how that Menelaus has not yet passed through murky Erebus, being hidden in the earth; but that, still worn down on the waves' of the sea, he has not yet touched the ports of his country land, wretched in his wandering of life, friendless of friends, upon all manner of lands drawing nigh his foot with the marine oar, from the Trojan land.　　418

HELEN

Hither I am come again to the seat of this tomb, having learned pleasing news from Theonoe; who knows all things truly. For she says that my husband, yet dwelling in the light, beholds the light, but wanders, having sailed through innumerable seas, hither and thither; and that he will come not unexercised in wanderings, when indeed he shall obtain an end of his troubles. But one thing she did not say, whether on his arrival he will be saved. But I stood off from clearly asking this, being delighted, since she said that he was preserved for me. And she said that he was some where near this land, having been cast shipwrecked with a few friends.

Ah! wilt thou come to me? How longed-for wouldst thou come! Ha! who is this? surely I am not stealthily attacked through the devices of the impious son of Proteus? Shall I not, like a swift foal, or Bacchanal of the God, unite my limbs with

the tomb? But this is some man, savage in appearance, who
seeks to take me.   434

MENELAUS
Oh thou who art striving forward with terrible hastening
to the base of the tomb and the burning cakes, remain; why
dost thou fly? How, after showing thy person to my view, dost
thou bring astonishment and an inability to speak!   437

HELEN
I am wronged, women; for I am kept off from the sepulchre
by this man; and he wishes, having seized me, to give me to
the tyrant from whose nuptials I fled.

MENELAUS
We are not thieves, nor ministers of bad men.   440

HELEN
And yet thou hast an unseemly garb around thy body.

MENELAUS
Stay thy swift foot, dismissing fear.

HELEN
I stay it, since indeed I touch this place.

MENELAUS
Who art thou? What sight, lady, do I behold in thee?

HELEN
And who art thou? for the same question possesses me.

MENELAUS
(Aside.)
I never saw a frame more like—   446

HELEN
(Aside.)
O Gods, for a God it is to recognize those dear

MENELAUS
Grecian art thou, woman, or one of the country?

HELEN
Grecian; but I also wish to know thy (country).

MENELAUS
I perceive thee, lady, most like to Helen.   450

HELEN
And I thee, indeed, to Menelaus; nor know I what to say.

MENELAUS
Thou hast well recognized a most ill-fortuned man.

HELEN
O thou who after a long time hast come into the hands of
thy wife!

MENELAUS
Of what wife? Touch thou not my garments.

HELEN
She whom Tyndarus my father gave thee.   455

MENELAUS
thou light-bearing Hecate, send favorable visions.

HELEN
In me thou beholdest not a night-seen minister of Hecate.

MENELAUS
No one man is born husband of two wives.

HELEN
And of what other marriage-bed arit thou the lord?

MENELAUS
(Of her) whom a cave hides, and (whom) I am carrying off
from the Phrygians.   460

HELEN
None other than myself is thy wife.

MENELAUS
Am I then in my senses, but mine eye at fault?

HELEN
For dost not thou, seeing me, think that thou seest thy
wife?

MENELAUS
Thy body is like (to hers); but clearness of decision is
wanting to me.   464

HELEN
Consider. But in this no man is a better judge than you.

MENELAUS
Thou art like (her). This at least I will not deny.

HELEN
Who other than thine eyes shall teach thee?

MENELAUS
In this 1 am at fault, that I have another wife.

HELEN
I came not to the Trojan land; but it was a spectre.

MENELAUS
And who makes bodies capable of sight?   470

HELEN
The ether; whence thou hast a wife made by a God.

MENELAUS
Which of the Gods was the moulder? for thou tellest
unexpected things.

HELEN
It was an exchange effected by Juno, that Paris might not
receive me.

MENELAUS
How then wast thou here and at Troy at the same time?

HELEN
My name might be in many places, but not my body.   475

MENELAUS
Let me go; 1 have come possessing griefs enough.

HELEN
What, wilt thou leave me, and bear away that vain spouse?

MENELAUS
Ay, and fore thee well, because thou art like Helen.

HELEN

I am undone; having found thee, I shall not possess a husband.

MENELAUS

The might of my labors there persuades me, not thou.   480

HELEN

Woe's me! Who was ever more wretched than I? Those dearest desert me, nor shall I ever come to the Greeks nor to my country.

MESSENGER
(Entering.)
Menelaus, after seeking thee, I find thee with difficulty, having wandered about the whole of this barbarian land, sent by thy surviving friends.   484

MENELAUS

What is the matter? Are ye plundered by the barbarians?

MESSENGER

(I am come), having a marvel (to tell of), less in name than in fact.

MENELAUS

Say; since by this haste (of thine) thou bearest some new tidings.

MESSENGER

I say that thou hast vainly undergone innumerable toils.

MENELAUS

Thou weepest ancient ills. But what is your news?   489

MESSENGER

Thy wife has departed to the folds of the sky, wafted from view; and she is hidden in heaven, having quitted the sacred cave, where we were guarding her, (and) having spoken thus much: "O miserable Phrygians, and ye all Greeks, through me, by the art of Juno, ye died at the banks of Scamander, thinking that Paris, who had not Helen, did have her. But I, after I had remained as long a time as it behooved me, preserving the decree of fate, will go to heaven my father; but the hapless daughter of Tyndarus has vainly borne evil reports, being in nothing guilty." O hail! thou daughter of Leda, thou wert here. But I told of thee as having gone to

the recesses of the stars, naught knowing that thou bearest
a winged body. I will not again permit thee to mock us; since
vainly at Troy didst thou give troubles to thy husband and
allies.   502

MENELAUS

This is it. The true words of this woman have come together.
longed-for day, that has given thee to me to receive in my
arms.

HELEN

O Menelaus, most dear of men, the time indeed is ancient,
but the pleasure is lately near at hand. With delight have I
received my husband, friends, throwing around (him) my loving
hand after a long lapse of light-bearing days.   507

MENELAUS

And I (embrace) thee; but having many things to tell of
common interest, I know not with which I now shall first
begin.

HELEN

I rejoice, and I, bird-like, am uplifted as to the hair
erect on my head," and I shed the tear (of joy). But around
thy limbs I cast my hands, now that I receive delight. O
husband, O sight most dear!   512

MENELAUS

I do not blame thee. I possess my wife, the daughter of
Jove and Leda, whom by lamplight her twin brothers on their
white steeds blessed, ah! blessed in former times; but the
Gods conveyed thee from me.   515

HELEN

But the deity leads on to another fortune better than this,
and evil has brought thee and me to good, O husband, after a
long season; but nevertheless may I enjoy my fortune.

MENELAUS

Mayest thou indeed enjoy; in this same prayer I join, for
of the two one cannot be wretched, the other not.

HELEN

My friends, my friends, we no longer mourn past evils, nor
do I grieve. I have, 1 have my husband, for whom I have
waited, waited to come for many a year.   520

MENELAUS
Thou hast me, and I have thee; but having with difficulty passed through numberless years, I perceive the plans of the Goddess. But my joyous tears have more of joy than grief.

HELEN
What can I say? Who of mortals would ever have hoped for this? I hold thee unexpected to my breast.

MENELAUS
And I thee, who wast thought to have come to the Idaean city and unhappy towers of Troy. By the Gods, bow wast thou removed from mine house?   525

HELEN
Alas! alas! to a bitter commencement thou art coming; alas! alas! and a bitter report art thou tracking.

MENELAUS
Speak; for all that is brought to pass by the Gods may be listened to.

HELEN
I abhor the story; what kind shall I introduce?

MENELAUS
Yet speak. Sweet is it in truth to hear of labors.   529

HELEN
Not to the couch of a barbarian youth with a flying oar, and with the winged love of lawless nuptials (did I go).

MENELAUS
For what deity, or what fortune robbed thee of thy country?

HELEN
The son of Jove, of Jove, O husband, has caused me to approach the Nile.

MENELAUS
Marvelous things (thou tellest) of the sender. O fearful tale!

HELEN
I have wept, and I now wet mine eyelids with tears. The wife of Jove has destroyed me.   535

MENELAUS
Juno? Desiring to add what of ills?

HELEN
Alas! for my woes, for the baths and fountains, where the
Goddesses beautified their forms, (and) where came the trial.

MENELAUS
Did Juno bring on thee these ills on account of that trial?

HELEN
(Ay), that she might take away love—

MENELAUS
How? Speak.   540

HELEN
From Paris, to whom (Venus) had by her nod given me.

MENELAUS
O wretched one.

HELEN
Wretched, wretched one! Thus she caused thee to approach
Egypt.

MENELAUS
Then she gave a phantom in thy stead, as I hear from you.

HELEN
But for the sufferings, the sufferings at home, mother,
woe is me!   545

MENELAUS
What sayest thou?

HELEN
My mother is no more. Through me, an ill-wedded disgrace!
she fastened the strangling noose.

MENELAUS
Ah me! And is thy daughter Hermione alive?

HELEN
Unwedded, childless, O husband, she with shame laments my
nuptials no nuptials.   550

MENELAUS
O Paris, who hast utterly destroyed my house, these things
have destroyed both thee and myriads of brazen-armed Greeks.

HELEN
But me, ill fated, accursed, the God cast out from my
country, from my city, and from thee, in that I, not leaving,
left thy house and couch for shameful nuptials.

CHORUS
If ye can meet with prosperous fortune hereafter, it will
avail against the past.   555

MESSENGER
Menelaus, to me also give some of the pleasure, which I
too am hearing, but do not clearly possess.

MENELAUS
Thou too, old man, share our discourse.

MESSENGER
Is not this the authoress of our troubles at Troy?

MENELAUS
Not she, we were deceived by the Gods, having a sad image
of vapor in our hands.

MESSENGER
What sayest thou? Did we then vainly undergo toils for a
cloud?   560

MENELAUS
This was the deed of Juno, and the strife of the three
Goddesses.

MESSENGER
And is this woman really and truly thy wife?

MENELAUS
Herself; believe this on my assertion.   563

MESSENGER
O daughter, how variable is the Deity, and inscrutable!
But well I ween he turns things around, bearing them hither
and thither. One man toils; another, who has not toiled, in
turn evilly perishes, possessing firmly nothing of his
fortune, which is only for the time being. For thou and thy

husband did share in troubles, thou indeed in words, but lie in his ardor for the deeds of the spear. But hastening, when he hastened he obtained naught, but now lie fares most fortunately, having obtained good spontaneously. Then thou hast not disgraced thy old father and the Dioscuri, nor hast thou done such things as are reported! Now I again renew the hymeneal rite, and call to mind the torches, which I bore, running beside the four-horsed chariot: and thou in thy car quitted thy happy home with this man as his bride. For base is that man who regards not his masters' affairs and does not rejoice and grieve together in their good and ill. May I, indeed, although born a servant, be numbered among generous slaves, not having the name, but the mind of a freeman. For better is this than, being one man, to be subject to two evils, both to have a bad disposition, and to be taunted by others as the slave of neighbors. 583

MENELAUS

Come, O aged man, many labors hast thou performed near my shield, having toiled through them with me; and now having shared in (the news of) my prosperity, go, tell the tidings to our surviving friends, how you have found these matters, and in what state of fortune we are. And (bid them) stay on shore, and wait for my contests that remain, and which I expect, and to keep watch (if) we can by any means steal away this woman from the land, in order that by coming to one point of luck, we may, if we can, be saved from the barbarians.

MESSENGER

These things shall be, O king. Although I have witnessed how trivial and how full of falsehoods are the words of seers. There is nothing sound in the flames of lire, nor in the voices of winged birds. And foolish indeed it is even to suppose that birds can benefit mortals. For neither Calchas said nor signified to the army, when he saw his friends dying on account of a cloud, nor Helenus; but the city was destroyed in vain. You will say it was because the deity did not wish it (that they should speak); why then do we consult seers? It behooves us, sacrificing to the Gods, to ask for good things, but to let alone prophecies. For this was invented as naught but a bait to life; and no one, being a sluggard, ever grew rich on divinations. For discernment and prudence are the best of prophets." 605

CHORUS

My opinion, too, concerning prophets tends to the same
point with this old man's. If one has the Gods as his friends,
he has the best divination in his house.   607

HELEN

Be it so. Thus far matters stand well; but to learn how
thou, O hapless man, wast saved from Troy, is indeed no
profit; but there is a certain desire for friends to hear the
troubles of friends.   610

MENELAUS

In truth thou hast asked me many things in a single sentence
and by a single road. Why should I tell thee of the shipwrecks
in the Aegean Sea, of the fires lighted in Euboea by Nauplius,
and of Crete, and of Libya, to which cities I turned my
course, and of the look-outs of Perseus. I could never satisfy
thee with the story, and telling thee my troubles I should
still grieve. In suffering I was troubled; and I should thus
be pained twice.   617

HELEN

Thou hast spoken more fitly than I asked thee. But, leaving
all (other matters), tell me one thing. For how long a time
hast thou been tossed in marine wanderings upon the surface
of the sea?   620

MENELAUS

Year after year in addition to the ten years at Troy, I
have passed through seven revolutions of years.

HELEN

Alas! alas! a long time thou tellest, O hapless one. And
being preserved from thence, thou art hither come to death.

MENELAUS

How sayest thou? What wilt thou say? How hast thou undone
me, woman!

HELEN

Thou wilt perish by the man whose house this is.

MENELAUS

Having done what deed worthy of this misfortune?   625

HELEN

Thou art come unexpected and a hinderance to my nuptials.

MENELAUS
What, has some one wished to wed my wife?

HELEN
Ay, and to work that insult on me, which I have undergone.

MENELAUS
Some one of private influence, or ruling the land?

HELEN
The son of Proteus, who governs this country.   630

MENELAUS
This is that riddle which I heard from the servant.

HELEN
Standing at what barbarian portals?

MENELAUS
These, from whence I was driven like a beggar.

HELEN
And wast thou craving sustenance? O wretched me!

MENELAUS
The matter indeed was such, but it had not this name.   635

HELEN
Thou knovest then, as you seem, all about my nuptials?

MENELAUS
I know; but this I know not, whether thou hast escaped the
nuptials?

HELEN
Know that thy bed has been preserved inviolate for thee.

MENELAUS
What evidence (is there) of this? for thou tellest pleasant
things, if true.

HELEN
Dost thou behold the unhappy seat of me a suppliant at this
tomb?   640

MENELAUS
I see a couch strewn on the ground, O wretched one; but what have you to do with it?

HELEN
Here I have kept beseeching an escape from nuptials.

MENELAUS
Through lack of an altar, or after barbarian customs?

HELEN
This has been defense for me equal to the temples of the Gods.

MENELAUS
Is it not then allowed me to ship thee homewards?   645

HELEN
The sword, rather than my bed, will await thee.

MENELAUS
Thus I shall be the most wretched of mortals.

HELEN
Do not then be ashamed (to flee), but escape from this land.

MENELAUS
Leaving thee? I have destroyed Troy for thy sake.

HELEN
For it is better than for my bed to cause your death.   650

MENELAUS
Thou speakest unmanly acts, and unworthy of Troy.

HELEN
Thou wilt not slay the king, as thou perhaps aimest at.

MENELAUS
Has he then a body invulnerable to the sword?

HELEN
Thou wilt see; but to dare what is impossible is not the part of a wise man.

MENELAUS
Shall I then in silence give him my hands to bind?   655

HELEN
Thou art come to a difficulty, and there is need of some contrivance.

MENELAUS
For better is it to die by doing than by not doing.

HELEN
There is one hope, by which alone we may be saved.

MENELAUS
To be purchased, or dared, or depending upon words?

HELEN
If the tyrant were not to hear of thy arrival.   660

MENELAUS
And who will tell (him) of me? He will not surely know who I am.

HELEN
Within he has an ally equal to the Gods.

MENELAUS
Some oracular voice shrined in his dwelling?

HELEN
No, but his sister; they call her Theonoe.

MENELAUS
A name for oracles; but say, what is she doing?   665

HELEN
She knows all, and will tell her brother thou art present.

MENELAUS
Then I shall die; for it is impossible for me to lie concealed.

HELEN
If we could both by any entreaties persuade her—

MENELAUS
To do what thing? Into what hope dost thou lead me?   669

                              HELEN
Not to tell her brother of your presence in the land?

                             MENELAUS
And having persuaded her, could we separate our footsteps
from the land?

                              HELEN
Easily, in common with her, but not by stealth.

                             MENELAUS
It is thy work; since a woman is fitted for a woman,

                              HELEN
She shall not have her knees untouched by my hands.

                             MENELAUS
But what if she will not receive our entreaties?   675

                              HELEN
Thou wilt die; and I unhappy shall be wedded by force.

                             MENELAUS
Thou wouldst be a traitress. Thou usest that force as a
pretense.

                              HELEN
But I have sworn a sacred oath by thine head.

                             MENELAUS
What sayest thou? that thou wilt die, and never change
thine husband?   679

                              HELEN
Ay, and with the same sword; and I will lie beside thee.

                             MENELAUS
On these terms touch then my right hand.

                              HELEN
I touch it, (swearing) that if thou diest, I will quit this
light.

                             MENELAUS
And I, deprived of thee, will end my life.

HELEN

How then shall we die, so as to obtain renown?   684

MENELAUS

Having slain thee on the back of the tomb, I will slay myself. But first we will engage in a mighty contest for thy bed; and let him who will, draw nigh. For I will not disgrace my renown at Troy; nor shall I returning to Greece obtain much reproach, who deprived Thetis of Achilles, and have seen the death of Ajax the son of Telamon, and the son of Neleus; but for my own wife's sake shall I not think fit to die? Ay, most decidedly, for if the Gods are wise, they will with light earth cover in the tomb the valiant man, who has fallen by the enemy, but cast the craven beneath a hard mound of earth.

CHORUS

O Gods, at length may the race of Tantalus be prosperous, and be freed from ills.   695

HELEN

Alas! me wretched. For thus am I in fortune, O Menelaus. We are undone. The prophetic Theonoe is coming out of the palace. The house resounds, as the bars are loosened. Fly; but how canst thou fly? For both absent and present she knows that thou hast come hither. O wretched one, how am I undone! For thou, after being preserved from Troy, and from a barbarian land, will, coming to barbarians' swords, fall again.   702

THEONOE
(Followed by two female attendants.)

Do thou indeed lead the way, bearing the light of lamps, and with sulphur purge the holy consecrated recess of the air, that we may receive the pure breath of heaven. And do thou in turn purify with cleansing flame the path, should any one have violated it, by treading with impious foot; and shake the pine-brand, that I may pass through. But both of you, having performed this law of mine, take back the flame of the hearth into the dwelling. Helen, what, how stand my divinations? Thy husband Menelaus is plainly come hither, deprived of his ships, and of thine image.   711

O wretched one, from what toils having escaped didst thou come, nor knowest whether thou wilt return home, or remain here. For there is a strife among the Gods; and a council concerning thee will be this day sitting near Jove. Juno, indeed, who before was hostile to thee, is now well inclined, and wishes to bring you safe to your country with this (your wife), that Greece may learn that the nuptials of Paris, the gift of Venus, were pretended nuptials. But Venus wishes to destroy thy return, that she may neither be convicted, nor be seen to have purchased (the palm of) beauty by a foolish marriage with Helen. But the result rests with me, whether, as Venus desires, having told my brother thou art here, I shall destroy thee; or, on the other hand, siding with Juno, I save thy life, concealing thee from my brother, who appoints me to tell him of this, when thou chancest to arrive at this land. Who will go to tell my brother that this man is here present, that I may be safe? 726

HELEN

O virgin, I fall a suppliant at thy knee, and am sitting at a seat not blest, both on my behalf and this man's, whom with difficulty at length having found, I am on the very point of seeing dying. Tell not to thy brother that this my husband is come into these most loving hands; but save him, I beseech thee; and for thy brother do not desert thy piety, purchasing base and unjust thanks. For the deity hates violence, and orders all men to obtain what may be acquired, not through plunder. For the heaven is common to all mortals, and the earth, on which it behooves us dwelling in our houses, not to have other men's goods, nor to seize them by force. But Hermes, by the will of heaven indeed, but sadly for me, has given me to thy father to preserve for this my husband; who is present and desires to take me away. 739

How then, dying, can lie take me away? And how could he ever restore the living: to the dead? Now consider the will of the deity and of thy sire, whether the deity and the deceased would wish or not wish to restore again the property of their neighbors. I think (they would). It behooves thee not to attach greater weight to thy silly-minded brother than thy good father. But if, being a prophetess, and believing there are Gods, thou shalt break through thy father's justice, and do favor to thine unjust brother, 'tis base indeed that thou shouldst know all things divine, what is, what is not, but not know things just. But deliver wretched me from the ills in which I lie, giving this as a by-deed of fortune; for there is no one among mortals who hates not Helen; I who am bruited through Greece as having betrayed my husband, and dwelt in the wealthy mansions of the Phrygians. But if I come to Greece, and again tread the land of Sparta, they hearing, (and) seeing, that it was by the contrivance of the Gods they perished, and that I was not the betrayer of my friends, will again on the contrary restore me to (the repute of) modesty, and I shall dower my daughter, whom no one marries; and quitting my bitter wanderings here, I shall enjoy the wealth that is in my house. But if indeed this man dying had been consumed on the funeral pile, I should with my tears have cherished him being far away; but shall I now be deprived of him, who is alive and well?   763

Not so, O virgin; but 1 implore thee this; grant me this favor, and imitate the manners of thy just sire. For this is the fairest renown for children, whosoever being sprung from a good father, arrives at the same manners as his parents.

CHORUS

Piteous indeed are the words just spoken, and pitiable too art thou. But I desire to hear from Menelaus what words he will speak on behalf of his life.   769

MENELAUS

I could not endure to fall prostrate at your knees, nor to bedew mine eyelids with tears; for, becoming a craven, I should very greatly disgrace Troy. And yet they say that it is the part of a man well born to shed the tear from his eyes in misfortunes. But not even this honorable act, if honorable it be, will I choose before a courageous soul. But if indeed it seems good to thee to save a stranger, and me who justly seeks to recover my wife, restore her, and moreover, save me; but if it does not seem good, I shall be not wretched now for the first time, but often (before), and thou wilt appear a wicked woman. But those things which we deem worthy of us, and just, and which will chiefly touch thine heart, I will gladly say near this monument of thy sire. thou old man, who dwellest in this stone tomb, restore (her).   782

I demand back of thee my wife, whom Jove sent hither for thee to preserve for me. I know that thou being dead canst never make us restitution, but this woman will not think fit that her father, who was once most glorious, should hear reproaches, being called upon from below, for she now has the power. O nether Hades, thee too I invoke as ally, who hast received for the sake of this woman many bodies that fell by my sword, and thou hast thy reward. Either then give them back again to life, or compel this woman who seems to be better than her impious sire, to give back my nuptials.   591

But if ye rob me of my wife, I will tell thee what arguments she has omitted. By an oath, O virgin, (that thou mayest know it,) we are bound first to do battle with thy brother; and he or I must die; the word is simple. But if he does not in the fight oppose foot to foot, but seeks (to slay) by starvation us suppliant at this tomb; it has been determined by me to slay this woman, and then to drive this two-edged sword to my heart, upon the summit of this tomb, that streams of blood may trickle down the burial-place; and we shall afterwards lie, two corses on this polished tomb, an undying grief to thee, and reproach to thy sire. For neither thy brother nor any one else shall wed this woman; but I will take her away for myself, if not to my house, at least to the dead. What is this? turning myself to woman by tears, I shall be an object of pity rather than a man to act. Slay, if please thee; for thou wilt not slay me ingloriously; but rather indeed be persuaded by my words, that thou mayest be just, and I may recover my wife.

808

CHORUS

It is for thee, O damsel, to decide the question. But do thou give judgment so as to please all parties.

THEONOE

I am both born to act piously, and willing to do so; and I love myself, and I would not stain the renown of my father; nor would I grant a favor to my brother by which I shall appear infamous. But in me there is by nature a great shrine of justice; and having this from Nereus, I will endeavor to preserve Menelaus. And since Juno wishes to benefit thee, I will place my vote on the same side; and may Venus be propitious to me, although she has never marched with me: and I will endeavor to remain a virgin for ever. But as to the matters of which thou hast spoken as a disgrace to my father at this tomb, there is the same language on my part. I should be guilty of injustice, should I not restore (thy wife); for he would, if living, have given back to her to possess thee, and thee to (possess) her. For in sooth there is vengeance for these matters both among the dead, and to all men above. The mind of the deceased lives not indeed, but has an immortal intelligence, falling into the immortal ether. That I may not, then, make a long speech, I will be silent as to the things thou hast besought me; nor in folly will I ever be a fellow counsellor with my brother; for I benefit him, though not seeming to do so, if from impiety I make him holy. Do ye then your-selves find out an escape; and I, getting out of the way, will keep silence. But begin ye from the Gods, and beseech Venus indeed to let thee return to thy country; and that Juno's resolves may remain in the same state, which she entertains for the safety of thee and thy husband. But thou, my deceased father, as far as I have strength, shalt never be called impious instead of pious.

837

(Exit THEONOE.)

CHORUS
No one, being born unjust, has ever prospered; but
injustice are there hopes of safety.

HELEN
Menelaus, we have been saved by the virgin; but
henceforward it behooves thee, producing reasons, to combine
a common contrivance for our safety.   840

MENELAUS
Hear then indeed. Thou hast long ben in the dwelling, and
hast been bred up with the attendants on the king.

HELEN
Why dost thou say this? for thou bringest hopes as though
about to do something for our common good.

MENELAUS
Couldst thou persuade any one of those who guide the four-
horse chariots, so as to furnish us with a car?

HELEN
I might persuade; but what flight can we take, being
ignorant of the plains and the barbarian land?   845

MENELAUS
You mention a thing impossible. Come; what if, hiding
myself in the house, I were to slay the king with this two-
edged sword?

HELEN
His sister would not suffer it, nor be silent, if thou wert
about to slay her brother.

MENELAUS
But neither is there a ship, in which flying we might be
saved, for the sea possesses the one we had.

HELEN
Listen, if even a woman can say aught wise. Art thou willing
to be reported dead in words, not being dead?   850

MENELAUS
'Tis a bad omen; but if I gain by saying so, I am ready to
die in report, not dying.

HELEN

And truly we will excite pity in the impious (king) by female cuttings of hair and groanings.

MENELAUS

But what means of safety does this furnish for us? For there is something of simplicity in the design.

HELEN

I will request the tyrant of this land to make a burial in an empty tomb, as though you had died by sea.   855

MENELAUS

And suppose he permits; how then shall we, having given an empty tomb to my body, be saved without a ship?

HELEN

I will urge him to bestow a ship, in which he will place adornments for thy coffin to be thrown into the arms of the deep.

MENELAUS

How well hast thou spoken of this, save in one thing, should he bid thee make the burial on the land! The pretense will bring nothing with it.

HELEN

But we will say that it is not the custom in Greece to inter on land those who die at sea.

MENELAUS

In this again thou art right; then shall I sail with thee, and place the adornments on board the same bark?   860

HELEN

It behooves thee especially to be present, and thy sailors, who escaped from the shipwreck.

MENELAUS

And truly if I lay hold of a ship at anchor, man shall stand by man sword in hand.

HELEN

It behooves thee to decide on all this. Only let there be escorting breezes to the sail, and to the ship a course.

MENELAUS

It will be so; for the Gods will put a stop to my troubles.
But from whom wilt thou say thou hast learnt I am dead?

HELEN

From thee. And do thou say that thou alone hast escaped
death, sailing with the son of Atreus, and that you saw him
perish.   866

MENELAUS

And truly these rags, the coverings of my body, will bear
witness concerning the wreck of the ships.

HELEN

(Things) have happened opportunely, which formerly were
inopportunely lost; and that unhappiness may perchance fall
out happily.

MENELAUS

But does it behoove me to enter the house with thee, or
shall we sit quiet at this tomb?   869

HELEN

Stay here; for even if he seek to do thee any wrong, this
tomb and thy sword will protect thee. But I, going into the
house, will shear my locks, and will exchange my white
garments for black. And on my cheek I will throw the nail,
(drawing) blood from the skin. For great is the struggle, and
I perceive two inclinations of the balance; for I must either
perish, if I be detected in my plans, or come to my country
and preserve thy life. O hallowed Juno, who reclinest on the
bed of Jove, give two unfortunate beings a rest from their
toils, we beseech thee, stretching our hands direct up to
heaven, where thou dwellest amid the varied spanglings of the
stars. And thou, who didst obtain (the prize of) beauty for
my nuptials, thou Venus, daughter of Dione, do not destroy
me. For enough is the injury, wherewith thou hast injured me
before, presenting among the barbarians my name, not my body.
But if thou wilt slay me, suffer me to die in father-land.
Wherefore art thou insatiate of ills, practising loves,
deceits, and cunning devices, and philters causing blood in
houses? But if thou wert moderate, in other respects thou art
the sweetest of Goddesses to men. I speak not in vain.   888

CHORUS

On thee I call, who sittest in thy seat of song beneath
the foliaged nooks; thee, the musical bird of sweetest

warbling, the plaintive nightingale. Come, O thou that through thy dun cheeks dost trill thy lay, a partner in my dirge, and singing the tearful toils of hapless Helen and of the Trojans under the spears of the Greeks; Paris, who came, who came to the plains (of Greece) with barbarian oar, who coursed the waves, bringing from Lacedaemon thy nuptials unhappy to the sons of Priam, when he had obtained (thee) by the gift of Venus. But many of the Greeks, having breathed out their life by the spear and hurlings of stones, possess sad Hades, having caused the mourning locks of their wives to be shorn; and dwellings exist without bridegrooms. But a man with a single bark having kindled up a burning flame, around sea-girt Euboea, (and) having fallen upon the Capherian rocks and the marine coasts of the Aegean, destroyed many, having lit up a deceitful light. But the mountains of Malea were without ports, when there rushed far from his country on the gale of the winds (a man) bearing in his ship in barbarian guise a prodigy, no prodigy, but strife on strife to the Greeks, a cloud, the divine image sent by Juno. Whether it was a God, or not a God, or something between, who of mortals can aver, having searched out to the. very end, so as to discover, who (indeed) perceives the counsels of the Gods flitting hither and thither in unexpected, contradictory turns of fate? 913

Thou art the daughter of Jove, O Helen, for thy winged sire begat thee in the bosom of Leda. And yet thy report through Greece is that of an unjust wretch, a betrayer, a faithless, godless one; nor have I (to say) what is clear among mortals. I find the word of the Gods to be true. Foolish ye, as many as obtain (the renown of) valor by war, foolishly resting from the toils of mortals in the spears of valiant war. For if the contest of blood is to determine (men's quarrels), never will strife leave the cities of men; which left the dwellings of the land of Priam, when it was in their power to decide by words the strife concerning thee, O Helen. But now they indeed are the care of Hades below, and fire, like the lightning of Jove, has fallen on their walls, bringing sufferings on sufferings in calamity to miserable Troy. 927

(Enter THEOCLYMENUS,
from hunting.)

THEOCLYMENUS

O hail, thou tomb of my sire; for I have interred thee at the outlets (of my palace) for the sake of my addressing it. For ever on going out and coming into the house, this thy son Theoclymenus addresses thee. Do ye indeed, O servants, remove the dogs and the nets for the wild beasts into the regal dwelling. But I indeed reproach myself much, in that we do not punish the bad with death. And now I learn that some one of the Greeks is openly come to this land, and has escaped the notice of the watch, either as a spy, or seeking to steal away Helen. But he shall die, if indeed he be but caught. Ha! I find, it seems, every thing evilly done; for the daughter of Tyndarus, having left empty her seat at the tomb, has been convoyed away from this land. Ho! open the doors, remove the horses from the stable, ye servants, and bring out the chariots, that, as far as trouble is concerned, the bride, whom I aim at, may not escape me, being carried off from this land. Stop I for I see her, whom I meant to pursue, present in the house, and not fled away. Thee I address. Why hast thou put black garments on thy form in exchange for white? and from thy noble head hast shorn the locks, having brought (upon them) the steel? and why art thou weeping and bedewing thy cheek with tears? Is it through being persuaded by nightly dreams that thou lamentest, or having heard some report from home art afflicted in thy mind with grief? 950

HELEN
My lord, for now I address you by this name, I am undone; my state is vanished, and I am nothing now.

THEOCLYMENUS
And in what state of calamity art thou? What has befallen?

HELEN
Menelaus, alas! how shall I say it?—is dead for me.

THEOCLYMENUS
I rejoice not indeed at thy words, but in some respects I am fortunate. How dost thou know? Does Theonoe tell thee this?

HELEN
Both she says so, and he who was present when he perished.

THEOCLYMENUS
What, has any one come, who tells this clearly? 957

HELEN
He has come. And may he come, as I should wish him to come.

THEOCLYMENUS
Who is it? Where is he? that I may learn more clearly?

HELEN
This man, who sits crouching at this tomb.   960

THEOCLYMENUS
Apollo! how conspicuous he is in unhappy garb!

HELEN
Alas! I fancy my husband too has such another.

THEOCLYMENUS
But of what country is this man, and whence has he come to
this land?

HELEN
A Greek, one of the Achaeans, a fellow-voyager with my
husband.

THEOCLYMENUS
By what death does he say Menelaus died?   965

HELEN
Most piteously, amid the wet surges of the main.

THEOCLYMENUS
Sailing where in the barbarian seas?

HELEN
Falling among the harborless rocks of Libya.

THEOCLYMENUS
And how did not this man perish, sharing in the ship?

HELEN
The worse are sometimes more fortunate than the good.   970

THEOOCLYMENUS
But where leaving the fragments of his ship, is he present?

HELEN
Where I wish he had perished, and not Menelaus.

THEOCLYMENUS
He is no more. But in what bark came (this man)?

HELEN
Sailors met with and took him up, as he says.   974

THEOCLYMENUS
Where indeed is the evil sent to Troy instead of thee?

HELEN
Thou meanest the image of cloud. It is gone to the sky.

THEOCLYMENUS
O Priam, and land of Troy, how vainly have ye perished!

HELEN
And I shared the calamity with the sons of Priam.

THEOCLYMENUS
But has she left her husband buried, or hides him in the earth!

HELEN
Unburied, alas! me wretched for mine ills.   980

THEOCLYMENUS
On this account hast thou shorn the locks of thy yellow hair?

HELEN
For he is dear, whoever he is, being here.

THEOCLYMENUS
Is this calamity rightly bewailed?

HELEN
Would it be a light thing for thy sister to die?   984

THEOCLYMENUS
No indeed. How then? Wilt thou still dwell at this tomb?

HELEN
Why dost thou mock me, and not leave alone the dead?

THEOCLYMENUS
Thou art faithful to thy husband, flying from me.

HELEN
But not so longer. Now begin my nuptials.

THEOCLYMENUS
Thou hast come (to this determination) late, but nevertheless I commend this.

HELEN
Knowest thou then what to do? Let us forget all that has
passed.   991

THEOCLYMENUS
On what condition? For let favor come in return for favor.

HELEN
Let us plight a truce, and be thou reconciled to me.

THEOCLYMENUS
I yield up my hostility to thee, and let it fly away.

HELEN
By thy knees then, since thou now art a friend—   995

THEOCLYMENUS
Seeking what thing, hast thou stretched out thyself as a
suppliant to me?

HELEN
I desire to inter my dead husband.

THEOCLYMENUS
But what interment is there for the absent? Wilt thou inter
his shade?

HELEN
It is a custom with the Greeks, whosoever dies at sea—

THEOCLYMENUS
To do what? The sons of Pelops in sooth are clever at such
things.   1002

HELEN
To bury in empty shrouds of vestments.

THEOCLYMENUS
Bury then. Raise a tomb where thou wilt in this land.

HELEN
We do not thus inter sailors who have perished.   1005

THEOCLYMENUS
How then? I am deficient in the customs of the Greeks.

HELEN

Into the sea we cast what are due to the dead.

THEOCLYMENUS

What then shall I furnish thee for the dead?

HELEN

I know not; for I am unskilled (in such matters), having before been happy.

THEOCLYMENUS

O stranger, thou hast indeed brought an acceptable message of words.   1010

MENELAUS

Not so to me indeed, or to the dead.

THEOCLYMENUS

How do ye inter the corses of those who die at sea?

MENELAUS

According as each person has means at hand.

THEOCLYMENUS

Speak in respect to expense, whatever you wish, for this woman's sake.

MENELAUS

The blood of a victim is first offered to the dead.   1015

THEOCLYMENUS

Of what victim? tell me, and I will comply.

MENELAUS

Decide thou thyself. For whatever thou shalt give, will suffice.

THEOCLYMENUS

Among the barbarians indeed the custom is a horse or bull.

MENELAUS

In giving it indeed, give thou nothing mean,

THEOCLYMENUS

We do not lack these (beasts) in our rich herds.   1020

MENELAUS
And biers empty of the body are brought (well) spread.

THEOOCLYMENUS
This shall be; but what other thing is it the custom to offer?

MENELAUS
Brazen-wrought arms; for he loved the spear.

THEOCLYMENUS
These, which we shall give, will be worthy the sons of Pelops.

MENELAUS
And the other beautiful fruits which the soil bears.   1025

THEOCLYMENUS
How then? In what way do ye cast them into the wave?

MENELAUS
A ship, and those who stand at the oar, must be present.

THEOCLYMENUS
And how far does the ship put out from land?

MENELAUS
So far, that the surge (around the keel) can scarcely be seen from land.

THEOCLYMENUS
Why indeed, and from what cause, does Greece respect this custom?
                                                         1030

MENELAUS
So that the waves may not cast the oblations back to land.

THEOOCLYMENUS
A swift-going Phoenician oar shall be furnished.

HELEN
It will be well, as a favor at least to Menelaus.

THEOOCLYMENUS
Wilt thou be sufficient to do these things without this (woman)?
                                                         1034

MENELAUS
This is the office of a mother, a wife, or of children.

THEOOCLYMENUS
It is the task of this woman, as you say, to inter her husband.

MENELAUS
It is piety at least not to rob the dead of their due.

THEOOCLYMENUS
Be it so; it is for my interest to train up a pious wife. But going into the house, I will bring forth adornments for the dead, and I will send thee away from the land not with empty hands, having done these things as a favor to this woman. But having brought me good tidings, instead of thy ragged garb thou shalt receive vesture and food, so as for thee to return to thy country, since indeed I see thee now in a wretched plight. But do thou, O wretched one, not for things which cannot be mended, away thyself. But Menelaus has his lot; for thy husband, being dead, can never live (again).

MENELAUS
'Tis thy task, O damsel. It indeed behooves thee to love thy present husband, but to let alone him that is dead, for this is best for thee under circumstances. But if I arrive in Greece, and obtain safety, I will cause thee to cease from thy former reproach, if thou be such a woman to thy consort as it becomes thee to be.   1051

HELEN
These things shall be, nor shall my husband ever find fault with me; but thou, being near, shalt thyself know this. But, O wretched one, go within, and obtain a bath, and change thy dress. "Without delay I will do thee a kindness; for thou wilt with better will perform the rites due to Menelaus, if thou meetest with such things from me as is befitting. 1056

CHORUS
Once on a time with hurried step the mountain-roaming mother of the Gods rushed through the woody groves, and the river-stream of waters, and the deep-roaring billows of the sea, in anxious desire of her departed daughter, not to be named. And the Bacchic cymbals sending forth a piercing clang, loudly shouted, when the Goddess, having yoked her chariot to wild beasts, (sought) her who had been snatched away from out the circles of virgin dances; and with (her) were damsels,

with feet as swift as the storm; Diana with her bow, and the
Gorgon in complete armor with her spear.   1065
   But (Jupiter), looking down from his heavenly (seat),
brought to pass another fate. But when the mother ceased from
her swift many-wandering toils, seeking out the stealthy
tracks of her daughter's abduction, she passed indeed the
snow-fed heights of the Idaean nymphs, and she casts (herself)
down in grief upon the rocky snow-covered thickets, and not
with ploughings fertilizing for mortals the plains of the
earth destitute of grass, she destroys the race of the people;
and sends not fresh pasture of rich-leaved tendrils for the
flocks. And the life of cities failed; and the sacrifices of
the Gods ceased, and cakes burned not on the altars, and she
stopped the dewy fountains of crystal waters from gushing
forth, raving through grief for her daughter. But when she
put a stop to the banquets of the Gods and of the human race,
Jove, softening the bitter wrath of the mother, said: "Go, ye
holy Graces, go, comfort with your voices the grief of Ceres
in wrath for her daughter; and ye Muses with the hymns of the
dance, and the skin-stretched drums with earthly sound of
brass.   1083
   Then first the fairest of the deities, the Goddess Venus,
both smiled, and received in her hands the deep-toned flute,
delighted with the strain. Him, whom it is neither lawful nor
pious, thou hast inflamed in marriage-beds (with love), and
thou, O daughter, hast obtained the wrath of the mighty
mother, not reverencing the sacrifices of the Gods. Of much
power indeed are the dappled skins of deer, and the green of
the ivy wound on the sacred wands, and the circular whirling
of the rhombus in the air, and the hair wildly dishevelled in
honor of Bacchus, and night-vigils for the Goddess. But well
did the Moon overcome her in the day. Thou alone prevailest
in beauty.   1094

                         HELEN
   In respect to matters in the house we are fortunate, O
friends; for the daughter of Proteus, who aids our escape,
having been asked about my husband being present has not told
her brother; but for my sake says that he, having died,
beholds no longer the light. Most beautiful arms indeed has
my husband snatched up; for the weapons he was about to let
down into the sea, these he himself bears, placing his noble
hand on the handle (of the shield), and taking the spear in
his right hand, as indeed jointly toiling in a favor to the
dead.   1103
   And before the deed he has his body equipped in arms for
battle, as being about to plant a trophy over numberless

barbarians by his hand, when we embark on the oared ship. And
having changed his shipwrecked dress for robes, I decked him
out, and gave his skin to the bath, a washing in the river
dew after a long time. But I must be silent; for he that
thinks he has my nuptials ready to his hands, is coming out
of the house; and we crave thy good will . . .   1110
        (To the CHORUS.)
. . . controlling thy tongue, that, if we can, ourselves
being saved, we may save thee also.

THEOCLYMENUS

Go forth in order, as the stranger directed, O servants,
bearing the marine burial offerings. O Helen, do thou, if I
seem not to speak ill to thee, be persuaded; remain here. For
being present thou wilt do the same things to thy husband as
if thou wert not present. For I fear lest some wild passion,
seizing thee, induce thee to cast thy body into the billows
of the sea, struck with the fond remembrance of thy former
spouse; for greatly dost thou bemoan him, though not present.

HELEN

O thou new husband mine, it is necessary to honor one's
first nuptials and marriage connections. But I, through
loving my husband, would even die with him. But what
gratification is it to him for me to die with the dead? Let
me then go myself and give a burial to his corse; and may the
Gods bestow what I wish on thee, and on this stranger, because
he aids me in this toil. But thou shalt have me such a wife
in your house as is fitting; since thou art benefiting
Menelaus and myself; for these matters indeed are coming to
a certain fortune. But command who is to give us a ship, in
which Ave may convey these things, that I may receive the
favor fully.   1130

THEOCLYMENUS
(To an ATTENDANT.)
Go then, and give to these a Sidonian ship of fifty oars,
and men to stand at the oars.

HELEN
Will not this man who adorns the tomb govern the ship?

THEOCLYMENUS
It particularly behooves my sailors to attend to him.

HELEN
Order it again, that they may clearly learn it from thee.

THEOCLYMENUS
Again I order it, ay, and a third time, if it is pleasing
to you.   1135

HELEN
Mayest thou profit (by it), and I by my plans.

THEOCLYMENUS
Do not now waste too much thy form with tears.

HELEN
This day to thee shall prove my gratitude.

THEOCLYMENUS
The matters of the dead are naught; but the labor is in
vain.

HELEN
There is both there and here of the things I mention.   1140

THEOCLYMENUS
Thou shalt find me no worse a husband than Menelaus.

HELEN
Thou art in naught to blame, it is the business of fortune
only.

THEOCLYMENUS
This rests with thee, if thou givest thy good-will to me.

HELEN
I shall not now be taught to love my friends.

THEOCLYMENUS
Dost thou wish that I myself, joining in the task, should
send out the expedition?   1145

HELENA
By no means. Be not a servant to thy servants, O King.

THEOCLYMENUS
Well then! I leave alone the laws of the sons of Pelops;
for my dwelling is pure; since Menelaus did not here breathe
out his life. But let some one go and tell my officers to
bear the bridal gifts into my palace. And it behooves the
whole land to resound with joyous hymns, the hymeneal song of
me and Helen, that it may be to be envied. But do thou, O

stranger, go and give to the arms of the sea these things in honour of the former husband of this woman. Again hasten to the house, having (with you) my wife, that, after you have enjoyed the nuptial feast of this lady with me, thou mayest set sail for thine home, or remaining, mayest be happy. 1156

MENELAUS

O Jove, thou art called both Sire and a wise God; look upon us, and remove us from our troubles. But strenuously assist us who are dragging our circumstances against a crag; and if you touch us with even the tip of your finger, we shall come to that pitch of fortune whither we fain would come. But enough of the labors we have before labored. Hear me, O Gods, that I may obtain many good things, free from pain. For I deserve not always to fare ill, but to walk with step erect. But bestowing one favor on me, ye will render me hereafter fortunate. 1165

CHORUS

O thou swift Phoenician oar of the Sidonian (ship), mother of frothy billows; thou that delightest in rowing, chorus-leader of the dolphins that gambol pleasantly, when the sea is quiet in its breezes, and the caerulean daughter of Ocean, Galaneia, thus speaks: " Stretch forth your sails, leaving them to the sea-breezes, and seize your oars of fir, O sailors! Ho! sailors, escorting Helen to the safe-harboring shores of the house of Perseus. Perchance thou mayest meet with the daughters of Leucippe by the river wave, or before the temple of Pallas, joining after a long season in the dances and revels of Hyacinthus, a nightly delight, with whom (Hyacinthus) Phoebus contending, unwillingly slew him with the quoit-end; whence the son of Jove ordered the Lacedaemonian land to hallow a day for the sacrifice of oxen; and the heifer, whom ye two left in your house . . . for whose nuptials the torches have not yet shone. Would that we might wing through the air, like Libyan birds in flocks, that quitting the winter storm, return, persuaded by the very old voice of their leader, who screams aloud, as he flies over the unwetted and fruitful plains of the land. O ye winged long-necked sharers of the course of the clouds, go ye beneath the middle Pleiads and nightly Orion, and proclaim the news, lighting on Eurotas, that Menelaus will return home, having captured the city of Dardanus. May ye come, O sons of Tyndarus, driving your horse-chariot through the sky, under the eddyings of the stars, ye who dwell in heaven, preservers of Helen, upon the dark-blue wave of the sea, and the caerulean foam of the waves whitening on the sea, sending to sailors gentle gales of winds from Jove. And avert from your sister the disgrace of barbarian nuptials, which she possessed, troubled on account of the Idaean contest, she who came not to the towers of Troy erected by Phoebus."   1196

MESSENGER

O king, we have found matters in the house in the worst state, so that thou wilt hear perhaps new troubles from me.

THEOCLYMENUS

But what is it?

MESSENGER

Seek the suitorship of another wife, for Helen has gone out of this land.   1199

THEOCLYMENUS

Raised aloft on winds, or with her foot treading the land?

MESSENGER

Menelaus, who himself came reporting his own death, has conveyed her away from the land.   1201

THEOOCLYMENUS

O thou who hast told dreadful things. And what guiding of a ship conveyed her from this land? for thou tellest incredible things.

MESSENGER

(The ship) indeed which thou gavest to the stranger; and he has gone away, having thine own sailors, that thou mayest briefly learn.

THEOOCLYMENUS

How? 1 am anxious to know; for I come not into the expectation that one single hand could overcome so many sailors, with whom thou wast sent.   1206

MESSENGER

When the daughter of Jove, after quitting this royal dwelling, went to the sea, most cleverly did she, placing her delicate step, bemoan her husband, though present, and not dead. But when we arrived at the enclosure of thy dockyards, we hauled out the best-sailing Sidonian ship, having a measure of fifty seats and oars, and work succeeded work. For one placed the mast, another the oar in his hand; and at the same time the white sails were (arranged), and at the same time the rudder let down with thongs. And during this labor some Grecian fellow-sailors, with Menelaus, watching for this very opportunity, drew nigh the shore, clad in the garb of shipwrecked mariners, of fair form indeed, but shabby to behold. But the son of Atreus, seeing them present, addressed them, alleging a feigned grief: "O unhappy men, how, and from what Grecian vessel are ye come, having shattered your bark? Will ye bury with me the dead son of Atreus, whom absent this, the daughter of Tyndarus, hononrs with an empty tomb? But they, shedding tears in a feigned guise, went on board the ship, bearing sea-offerings to Menelaus. But to us indeed this was suspicious; and (we said) to each other, that there was a multitude of those that came on board; yet we kept silence, obeying thy orders; for having commanded that the stranger should rule the ship, thou hast caused all this confusion. And the other things indeed we easily raised and placed within the ship; but the foot of the bull would not advance steadily along the gangway, but he bellowed, rolling around his eyes; and curving his back, and louring between his horns, he kept us off from touching him. But the husband of Helen called out: "O ye that did ravage the city of Troy, will ye not rush on, in Grecian manner, and seizing on your youthful shoulders heave the body of the bull up to the prow, (and at the same time he drew his sword,) an offering to the dead?" ¹²³⁸

And they, coming at his bidding, seized on the bull, and bearing it, they placed it on planks. And Menelaus, stroking down the neck and forehead of the bull with a single band, persuaded it to embark on the ship. At length, when the ship had received all things, Helen, having completed the number of the ladder's steps with her fair-ankled foot, sate down on the mid-deck, and near her Menelaus, in word indeed no longer living; but the rest of the crew in equal numbers on the right and left, man sate by man, having their swords concealed under their garments; and the waves were filled with the shouts, as we heard the voice of the boatswain. But when we had got out neither very far from, nor near to, the land, thus asked the guardian of the helm: " Shall we sail further onward, stranger, or is it well? for the government of the ship is thy charge." But he replied, "Enough for me." Drawing then his sword with his right hand, he went to the prow, and while he stood over the neck of the bull, of no one dead indeed had he a remembrance, but, as he cut the throat, he prayed: "O thou that dwellest in the seas, thou Ocean Neptune, and ye pure daughters of Nereus, preserve me and my wife inviolate from this land to the Nauplian shore." But a stream of blood darted into the wave, propitious to the stranger. And some one said: "This voyage is treacherous, let us sail back to Naxia; do thou give the command, and do thou turn the rudder." But after the slaughter of the bull the son of Atreus, standing up, called out to his allies: "Why delay ye, flower of the land of Greece, to slay, to kill the barbarians, and to cast them from the ship into the waves?" But to thy sailors the boatswain shouts acontrary cry; "Will ye not on? will not one seizing a remaining plank, another having broken a bench, and another tearing an oar from its row-lock, make bloody the head of these hostile strangers?" And they all jumped up erect, one party having ship's spars in their hands, but the other swords. And the ship streamed with gore. But there was the cheering cry of Helen from the prow, "Where is the renown of Troy? Show it against barbarian men."   1273

And in their haste they fell, and some rose up (again); but others thou mightest have seen lying dead. But Menelaus, equipped in arms, watching wherever his allies were troubled, bore thitherward the sword in his right hand, so that they dived from the ship, and he caused the oars to be deserted by thy sailors; and going to the helm, the king bade them guide the ship for Greece. And they raised the mast, and favorable gales sprang up, and they are gone from the land. But I, escaping death, let myself down into the sea near the anchor. And as my strength began to fail, some one, stretching forth a rope, drew me up, and landed me on shore to bear this news to thee. But there is naught more useful to mortals than a wise distrust.   1285

CHORUS
I never thought, O king, that Menelaus could thus have deceived thee and us, as he has deceived us, being present.

THEOOCLYMENUS
O wretched me, taken in a woman's toils, my nuptials have fled from me. But if indeed the ship could be taken by pursuit, I would have toiled and perchance caught the strangers. But now I will revenge myself on my sister, who has deceived me; for, seeing Menelaus in the house, she told me not. Never then shall she deceive another man by her prophecies.   1292

CHORUS
Ho thou! whither art thou stirring thy foot, O master; to what deed of blood?

THEOCLYMENUS
Whither justice bids me. But get out of the way.

CHORUS
I will not let go thy garments, for thou hastenest to great
evils.   1295

THEOOCLYMENUS
But wilt thou rule thy masters, being a slave?

CHORUS
Yes; for I am wise—

THEOCLYMENUS
But not for me, if ye will not let me go—

CHORUS
I will not then let thee go—

THEOCLYMENUS
To slay my most base sister—   1300

CHORUS
But yet most pious.

THEOCLYMENUS
Who has betrayed me?

CHORUS
An honorable betrayal, to do just deeds.

THEOCLYMENUS
Giving my bride to another?

CHORUS
To one who had a greater right.   1305

THEOOCLYMENUS
But who has a right over mine?

CHORUS
He who received her from her sire.

THEOCLYMENUS
But fortune gave her to me.

CHORUS
And fate has taken her away.

THEOCLYMENUS
Thou hast no right to judge of my affairs.   1310

CHORUS
Yes; if I speak better.

THEOCLYMENUS
We are governed; do not govern!

CHORUS
Ay, to do holy acts; but not unjust.

THEOCLYMENUS
Thou seemest to have a wish to die.   1314

CHORUS
Kill me, but thou shalt not kill thy sister with our
consent, but myself; since to generous servants it is most
glorious to die for their masters.   1316

CASTOR and POLLUX
(Appearing.)
Restrain the passion by which thou art not rightly hurried
on, Theoclymenus, king of this land. We, who call on thee,
are the twin sons of Jove, whom Leda once bore, with Helen,
who has fled from thine house. For thou art wrath about a
marriage not fated for thee; nor does the virgin, sprung from
the Goddess daughter of Nereus, thy sister Theonoe, do thee
wrong, honoring the will of the Gods, and her father's just
commands.   1323
For up to the now present time it was destined that she
should always dwell in thine house. But after the foundations
of Troy have been overturned, and she has furnished her name
to the Gods, it no longer behooves her to be yoked in the
same nuptials, but to arrive at her home, and dwell together
with her husband. But do thou keep off the black sword from
thy sister, and consider that she has done these things
prudently. Now we have long since (endeavored to) preserve
our sister even before this, ever since Jove made us Gods;
but we were too weak for fate and the Gods at once, to whom
it seemed fit that matters should be thus. To thee indeed I
speak thus; but to my sister I enjoin, "Sail with thy husband;
and ye shall have a favorable wind; and we, thy twin brothers,
riding by you over the main, will preserve and send you to
your country.   1337
But when thou shalt have turned (the course) and ended thy
life, thou shalt be called a Goddess, and with the Dioscuri

share libations, and with us receive gifts from men; for thus
Jove wills. But where first the son of Maia lodged thee,
having removed thee from Sparta, having from the abodes of
heaven stolen (an image of) thy person, lest Paris should
marry thee, there stretches a guard-coast territory along
Acte, I mean the island, that shall hereafter, among mortals,
be called Helene. And by the Gods it is destined for the
wanderer Menelaus to inhabit the islands of the blessed; for
the Gods do not detest the noble; but toils are rather for
the countless multitude.   1348

THEOOCLYMENUS

O ye twin sons of Jove and Leda, I will indeed let go my
former wrath concerning your sister; and I will not slay my
sister. But let her go to her home, if it please the Gods.
But know ye both that ye are born from the same kindred blood
as the best and chastest of sisters. And fare ye well, for
the sake of your most noble sister's mind, which is not in
the nature of many women.   1354

CHORUS

Many are the forms of things connected with the deities,
and many things the Gods perform contrary to our expectations.
But those things which we looked for are not accomplished;
but the God hath brought to pass things not looked for. Thus
has this matter turned out.   1358

(Exit.)

(LIGHTS FADE.)

(CURTAINS.)

(END OF PLAY.)

THE PHOENICIAN VIRGINS

THE PHOENICIAN VIRGINS

PERSONS REPRESENTED

JOCASTA

TUTOR

ANTIGONE

CHORUS OF PHOENICIAN VIRGINS

POLYNICES

ETEOCLES

CREON

MENCECEUS

TIRECIAS

MESSENGERS

OEDIPUS

THE ARGUMENT

Eteocles having gotten possession of the throne of Thebes, deprived his brother Polynices of his share; but he having come as an exile to Argos, married the daughter of the king Adrastus; but ambitious of returning to his country, and having persuaded his father-in-law, he assembled a great army for Thebes against his brother. His mother Jocasta made him come into the city, under sanction of a truce, and first confer with his brother respecting the empire. But Eteocles being violent and fierce from having possessed the empire, Jocasta could not reconcile her children.—Polynices, prepared as against an enemy, rushed out of the city. Now Tiresias prophesied that victory should be on the side of the Thebans, if Menoeceus the son of Creon would give himself up to be sacrificed to Mars. Creon refused to give his son to the city, but the youth was willing, and, his father pointing out to him the means of flight and giving him money, he put himself to death.—The Thebans slew the leaders of the Argives. Eteocles and Polynices in a single combat slew each other, and their mother having found the corses of her sons laid violent hands on herself; and Creon her brother received the kingdom. The Argives defeated in battle retired. But Creon, being morose, would not give up those of the enemy who had fallen at Thebes, for sepulture, and exposed the body of Polynices without burial, and banished Oedipus from his country; in the one instance disregarding the laws of humanity, in the other giving way to passion, nor feeling pity for him after his calamity.

SCENE: Court before the royal palace
                         at Thebes.

JOCASTA

O thou that cuttest thy path through the constellations of heaven, and art mounted on thy golden-joined seats, thou sun, whirling thy flame with thy swift steeds, how inauspicious didst thou dart thy ray on that day when Cadmus came to this land having left the sea-washed coast of Phoenicia; who in former time having married Harmonia, daughter of Venus, begat Polydorus; from him they say sprung Labdacus, and from him Laius. But I am the daughter of Menoeceus, and Creon my brother was born of the same mother; me they call Jocasta (for this name my father gave me), and Laius takes me for his wife; but after that he was childless, for a long time sharing my bed in the palace, he went and enquired of Apollo, and at the same time demands the mutual offspring of male children in his family; but the God said, "O king of Thebes renowned for its chariots, sow not for such an harvest of children against the will of the Gods, for if thou shalt beget a son, he that is born shall slay thee, and the whole of thy house shall wade through blood."   17

But having yielded to pleasure, and having fallen into inebriety, he begot to us a son, and having begot him, feeling conscious of his error and the command of the God, gives the babe to some herdsmen to expose at the meads of Juno and the rock of Cithaeron, having bored sharp-pointed iron through the middle of his ankles, from which circumstance Greece gave him the name of Oedipus. But him the grooms who attend the steeds of Polybus find and carry home, and placed him in the arms of their mistress. But she rested beneath her bosom him that gave me a mother's pangs, and persuades her husband that she had brought forth. But now my son showing signs of manhood in his darkening cheek, either having suspected it by instinct, or having learned it from some one, went to the temple of Apollo, desirous of discovering his parents; at the same time went Laius my husband, seeking to gain intelligence of his son who had been exposed, if he were no longer living; and both met at the same point of the road at Phocis where it divides itself; and the charioteer of Laius commands him, "Stranger, withdraw out of the way of princes;" but he moved slowly, in silence, with haughty spirit; but the steeds with their hoof dyed with blood the tendons of his feet.   38

At this (but why need I relate each horrid circumstance besides the deed itself?) the son kills his father, and having taken the chariot, sends it as a present to his foster-father

Polybus. Now at this time the sphinx preyed vulture-like upon the city with rapacity, my husband now no more, Creon my brother proclaims that he will give my bed as a reward to him who would solve the enigma of the crafty virgin.   45

But by some chance or other Oedipus my son happens to discover the riddle of the sphinx, (and he receives as a prize the sceptre of this land,) and marries me, his mother, wretched he not knowing it, nor knew his mother that she was lying down with her son. And I bear children to my child, two sons, Eteocles and the illustrious Polynices, and two daughters, one her father named Ismene, the elder I called Antigone.   52

But Oedipus, after having gone through all sufferings, having discovered in my bed the marriage with his mother, he perpetrated a deed of horror on his own eyes, having drenched in blood their pupils with his golden buckles. But after that the cheek of my children grows dark with manly down, they hid their lather confined with holts that his sad fortune might be forgotten, which indeed required the greatest policy. He is still living in the palace, but sick in mind through his misfortunes he imprecates the most unhallowed curses on his children, that they may share this house with the sharpened sword. But these two, dreading lest the Gods should bring to completion these curses, should they dwell together, in friendly compact determined that Polynices the younger son should first go a willing exile from this land, but that Eteocles remaining here should hold the sceptre for a year, changing in his turn; but after that he sat on the throne of power, he moves not from his seat, but drives Polynices an exile from this land. But he having fled to Argos, and having contracted an alliance with Adrastus, assembles together and leads a vast army of Argives; and having marched to these very walls with seven gates he demands his father's sceptre and his share of the land.   73

But I to quell this strife persuaded my son to come to his brother, confiding in a truce before he grasped the spear. And the messenger who was sent declares that he will come. But, thou that inhabitest the shining clouds of heaven, Jove, preserve us, give reconciliation to my children; it becomes thee, if thou art wise, not to suffer the same man always to be unfortunate.   79

TUTOR, ANTIGONE

TUTOR

O thou fair bud in thy father's house, Antigone, since thy
mother has permitted thee to leave the virgin's apartments
for the extreme chamber of the mansion, in order to view the
Argive army in compliance with thy entreaties, yet stay, until
I shall first investigate the path, lest any citizen should
appear in the pass, and to me taunts should come as a slave,
and to thee as a princess: and I who well know each
circumstance will tell you all that I saw or heard from the
Argives, when I went bearing the offer of a truce to thy
brother, from this place thither, and again to this place
from him. But no citizen approaches this house; come, ascend
with thy steps these ancient stairs of cedar, and survey the
plains, and by the streams of Ismenus and Dirce's fount how
great is the host of the enemy.   92

ANTIGONE

Stretch forth now, stretch forth thine aged hand from the
stairs to my youth, raising up the steps of my feet.

TUTOR

Behold, join thy hand, virgin, thou hast come in lucky
hour, for the Pelasgian host is now in motion, and they are
separating the bands from one another.   95

ANTIGONE

O awful daughter of Latona, Hecate, the field all brass
gleams like lightning.

TUTOR

For Polynices hath not come tamely to this land, raging
with host of horsemen, and ten thousand shields.

ANTIGONE

Are the gates fastened with bars, and is the brazen bolt
fitted to the stone-work of Amphion's wall?

TUTOR

Take courage; as to the interior the city is safe. But view
the first chief, if thou desirest to know.   100

ANTIGONE

Who is he with the white-plumed helmet, who commands in
the van of the army, moving lightly round on his arm his
brazen shield?

TUTOR

He is a leader, lady.

ANTIGONE

Who is he? From whom sprung? Speak, aged man, what is lie called by name?

TUTOR

He indeed is called by birth a Mycenaean, and he dwells at the streams of Lerna, the king Hippomedon.   105

ANTIGONE

Ah! how haughty, how terrible to behold! like to an earth-born giant, starlike in countenance amidst his painted devices, he corresponds not with the race of mortals.

TUTOR

Dost thou not see him now passing the stream of Dirce, a general?

ANTIGONE

Here is another, another fashion of arms. But who is he?

TUTOR

He is the son of Oedipus, Tydeus, and bears on his breast the Aetolian Mars.   110

ANTIGONE

Is this the prince, O aged man, who is husband to the sister of my brother's wife ? In his arms how different of color, of barbaric mixture!

TUTOR

For all the Aetolians, my child, bear the target, and hurl with the lance, most certain in their aim.

ANTIGONE

But how, O aged man, dost thou know these things so perfectly?

TUTOR

Having seen the devices of the shields, then I remarked them, when I went to bear the offer of a truce to thy brother, beholding which, I recognize the warriors.   116

ANTIGONE

But who is this, who is passing round the tomb of Zethus, with clustering locks, in his eyes a Gorgon to behold, in appearance a youth?

TUTOR

A general he is.

ANTIGONE

How a crowd in complete armor attends him behind?   120

TUTOR

This is Parthenopaeus, son of Atalanta.

ANTIGONE

But, may Diana who rushes over the mountains with his mother destroy him, having subdued him with her arrows, who has come against my city to destroy it.

TUTOR

May it be so, my child, nevertheless they are come with justice to this land; wherefore also I fear lest the Gods should judge rightly.   125

ANTIGONE

Where, but where is he who was born of one mother with me in hard fate, O dearest old man; tell me, where is Polynices?

TUTOR

He is standing near the tomb of the seven virgin daughters of Niobe, close by Adrastus. Seest thou him?

ANTIGONE

I see indeed, but not distinctly; but somehow I see the resemblance of his form, and his shape shadowed out. Would that with my feet I could perform the journey of the winged cloud through the air to my brother, then would I fling my arms round his dearest neck, after so long a time a wretched exile. How splendid is he, O old man, in his golden armor, glittering like the morning rays of the sun.   134

TUTOR

He will come to this house confiding in the truce, so as to fill thee with joy.

ANTIGONE

But who, O aged man, is this, who guides his milk-white steeds seated in his chariot?

TUTOR

The prophet Amphiaraus this, ray mistress, and with him the victims, the libations of the earth delighting in blood.

ANTIGONE

O thou daughter of the brightly girded sun, thou moon, golden-circled light, applying what quiet and temperate blows to his steeds does he direct his chariot! But where is he who utters such dreadful insults against this city, Capaneus?

TUTOR

He is scanning the approach to the towers, measuring the walls both from their foundation to the top.   143

ANTIGONE

O vengeance, and ye loud-roaring thunders of Jove, and thou blasting fire of the lightning, do thou quell this more-than-mortal arrogance. This is he who will with his spear give to Mycenae, and to the streams of Lernaean Triaena, and to the Amymonian waters of Neptune, the Theban women, having invested them with slavery. Never, O awful Goddess, never, O daughter of Jove, with golden clusters of ringlets, Diana, may I endure servitude.   150

TUTOR

My child, enter the palace, and at home remain in thy virgin chambers, since thou hast arrived at the indulgement of thy desire, as to what you were anxious to behold. For, since confusion has entered the city, a crowd of women is advancing to the royal palace. The race of women is prone to complaint, and if they find but small occasion for words, they add more, and it is a sort of pleasure to women, to speak nothing well-advised one of another.   157

CHORUS

I have come, having left the Tyrian wave, the first-fruits of Loxias, from the sea-washed Phoenicia, a slave for the shrine of Apollo, that I might dwell under the snowy brows of Parnassus, having sped my way over the Ionian flood by the oar, the west wind with its blasts riding over the barren plains of waters which flow round Sicily, the sweetest murmur in the heavens. Chosen out from my city the fairest present to Apollo, I came to the land of the Cadmeans, the illustrious descendants of Agenor, sent hither to these kindred towers of Laius. And I am made the slave of Apollo in like manner with the golden-framed images. Moreover the water of Castalia awaits me, to lave the virgin pride of my tresses, in the ministry of Apollo. blazing rock, the flame of fire that seems double above the Dionysian heights of Bacchus, and thou vine, who distillest the daily nectar, producing the fruitful cluster from the tender shoot; and ye divine caves of the dragon, and ye mountain watch-towers of the Gods, and thou hallowed snowy mountain, would that I were the chorus of the immortal God free from alarms encompassing thee around, by the caves of Apollo in the centre of the earth, having left Dirce. But now impetuous Mars having advanced before the walls lights up against this city, which may the Gods avert, hostile war; for common are the misfortunes of friends, and common is it, if this land defended by its seven turrets should suffer any calamity, to the Phoenician country, alas! alas! common is the affinity, common are the descendants of Io bearing horns; of which woes I have a share. 183

But a thick cloud of shields glares around the city, the likeness of gory battle, bearing which destruction from the Furies to the children of Oedipus Mars shall quickly advance. Pelasgian Argos, I dread thy power, and vengeance from the Gods, for he rushes not his arms to this war unjustly, who seeks to recover his home. 188

POLYNICES, CHORUS

POLYNICES

The bolts indeed of the gate-keepers have with ease admitted me, that I might come within the walls; wherefore also I fear, lest, having caught me within their nets, they let not my body go without bloodshed. On which account my eye must be turned about on every side, both that way and this, lest there be treachery. But armed in my hand with this sword, I will give myself confidence of daring. Ha! Who is this; or do we fear a noise? Every thing appears terrible even to the bold, when his foot shall pass across a hostile country. I trust however in my mother, at the same time I scarce trust, who persuaded me to come hither confiding in a truce. But protection is nigh; for the hearths of the altars are at hand, and houses not deserted. Come, I will let go my sword into its dark scabbard, and will question these who they are, that are standing at the palace. Ye female strangers, tell me, from what country do ye approach Grecian habitations? 203

CHORUS

The Phoenician is my paternal country, she that nurtured me: and the descendants of Agenor sent me hither from the spoils, the first-fruits to Apollo. And whilst the renowned son of Oedipus was preparing to send me to the revered shrine, and to the altars of Phoebus, in the mean time the Argives marched against the city. But do thou in turn answer me, who thou art, who hast come to this bulwark of the Theban land with its seven gates. 210

POLYNICES

My father is Oedipus the son of Laius; Jocasta daughter of Menoeceus brought me forth; the Theban people call me Polynices.

CHORUS

O thou allied to the sons of Agenor, my lords, by whom I was sent, I fall at thy knees in lowly posture, O king, preserving my country's custom. Thou hast come, thou hast come, after a length of time, to thy paternal land. O venerable matron, come forth quickly, open the doors; dost thou hear, O mother, that producedst this hero? why dost thou delay to leave thy lofty mansion, and to embrace thy child with thine arms? 219

JOCASTA, POLYNICES, CHORUS

JOCASTA

Hearing the Phoenician tongue, ye virgins, within this mansion, I drag my steps trembling with age. Ah! my son, after length of time, after numberless days, I behold thy countenance; clasp thy mother's bosom in thine arms, threw around her thy kisses, and the dark ringlets of thy clustering hair, shading my neck. Ah! scarce possible is it that thou appearest in thy mother's arms so unhoped for, and so unexpected. How shall I address thee? how shall I perform all? how shall I, walking in rapture around thee on that side and this, both with my hands and words, reap the varied pleasure, the delight of my former joys? O my son, thou hast left thy father's house deserted, sent away an exile by wrongful treatment from thy brother. How longed for by thy friends! how longed for by Thebes! From which time I am both shorn of my hoary locks, letting them fall with tears, with wailing; deprived, my child, of the white robes, I receive in exchange around me these dark and dismal weeds. 235

But the old man in the palace deprived of sight, always preserving with tears regret for the unanimity of the brothers which is separated from the family, has madly rushed on self-destruction with the sword and with the noose above the beams of the house, bewailing the curse imprecated on his children; and with cries of woe he is always hidden in darkness. But thou, my child, I hear, art both joined in marriage, and hast the joys of love in a foreign family, and cherishest a foreign alliance; intolerable to this thy mother and to the aged Laius, the woe of a foreign marriage brought upon us. But neither did I light the torch of fire for you, as is customary in the marriage rites, as befits the happy mother; nor was Ismenus careful of the bridal rites in the luxury of the bath: and the entrance of thy bride was made in silence through the Theban city. May these ills perish, whether the sword, or discord, or thy father is the cause, or whether fate has rushed with violence upon the house of Oedipus; for the weight of these sorrows has fallen upon me.   252

CHORUS
Parturition with the attendant throes has a wonderful effect on women; and somehow the whole race of women have strong affection towards their children.   254

POLYNICES
My mother, determining wisely, and yet not determining wisely, have I come to men my foes; but it is necessary that all must be enamored of their country; but whoever says otherwise, pleases himself with vain words, but has his heart there. But so far have I come to trouble and terror, lest any treachery from my brother should slay me, so that having my hand on my sword I proceeded through the city rolling round my eye; but one thing is on my side, the truce and thy faith, which has brought me within my paternal walls: but I have come with many tears, after a length of time beholding the courts and the altars of the Gods, and the schools wherein I was brought up, and the fount of Dirce, from which banished by injustice, I inhabit a foreign city, having a stream of tears flowing through my eyes. But, for from one woe springs a second, I behold thee having thy head shorn of its locks, and these sable garments; alas me! on account of my misfortunes. How dreadful a thing, mother, is the enmity of relations, having means of reconciliation seldom to be brought about! For how fares the old man my father in the palace, vainly looking upon darkness; and how fare my two sisters? Are they indeed bewailing my wretched banishment?

JOCASTA

Some God miserably destroys the race of Oedipus; for thus began it, when I brought forth children in that unhallowed manner, and thy father married me in evil hour, and thou didst spring forth. But why relate these things? What is sent by the Gods we must bear. But how I may ask the questions I wish, I know not, for I fear lest I wound at all thy feelings; but I have a great desire. 280

POLYNICES

But enquire freely, leave nothing out. For what you wish, my mother, this is dear to me.

JOCASTA

I ask thee therefore, first, for the information that I wish to obtain. What is the being deprived of one's country, is it a great ill?

POLYNICES

The greatest: and greater is it in deed than in word. 285

JOCASTA

What is the reason of that? What is that so harsh to exiles?

POLYNICES

One thing, and that the greatest, not to have the liberty of speaking.

JOCASTA

This that you have mentioned belongs to a slave, not to give utterance to what one thinks.

POLYNICES

It is necessary to bear with the follies of those in power.

JOCASTA

And this is painful, to be unwise with the unwise. 290

POLYNICES

But for interest we must bend to slavery contrary to our nature.

JOCASTA

But hopes support exiles, as report goes.

POLYNICES
They look upon them with favorable eyes, at least, but are slow of foot.

JOCASTA
Hath not time shewn them to be vain?

POLYNICES
They have a certain sweet delight to set against misfortunes.   295

JOCASTA
But whence wert thou supported, before thou foundest means of sustenance by thy marriage?

POLYNICES
At one time I had food for the day, at another I had not.

JOCASTA
And did the friends and hosts of your father not assist you?

POLYNICES
Be prosperous, and thou shah have friends; but friends are none, should one be in adversity.   299

JOCASTA
Did not thy noble birth raise thee to great distinction?

POLYNICES
To want is wretched; high birth fed me not.

JOCASTA
Their own country, it appears, is the dearest thing to men.

POLYNICES
You cannot express by words how dear it is.

JOCASTA
But how earnest thou to Argos? What intention hadst thou?

POLYNICES
Apollo gave a certain oracle to Adrastus.   305

JOCASTA
What is this thou hast mentioned? I am unable to discover.

POLYNICES
To unite his daughters in marriage with a boar and a lion.

JOCASTA
And what part of the name of beasts belongs to you, my son.

POLYNICES
I know not. The God called me to this fortune.

JOCASTA
For the God is wise. But in what manner didst thou obtain
her bed?   310

POLYNICES
It was night; but I came to the portals of Adrastus.

JOCASTA
In search of a couch to rest on, as a wandering exile?

POLYNICES
This was the case, and then indeed there came a second
exile.

JOCASTA
Who was this? how unfortunate then was he also!

POLYNICES
Tydeus, who they say sprung from Oedipus his sire.   315

JOCASTA
In what then did Adrastus liken you to beasts.

POLYNICES
Because we came to blows for lodging.

JOCASTA
In this the son of Talaus understood the oracle.

POLYNICES
And gave in marriage to us two his two virgin daughters.

JOCASTA
Art thou fortunate then in thy marriage alliance, or
unfortunate?   320

POLYNICES
My marriage cannot be found fault with up to this day.

JOCASTA

But how didst thou persuade an army to follow you hither?

POLYNICES

Adrastus swore this oath to his two sons-in-law, that he would replace both in their own country, but me first. And many princes of the Argives and Mycenaeans are at hand, rendering to me a sad, but necessary favor; for I am leading an army against this my own city; but I have called the Gods to witness how unwillingly I have raised the spear against my dearest parents. But the dissolution of these ills extends to thee, my mother, that having reconciled the friendly brothers, you may free from toil me and thyself, and the whole city. It is a proverb long ago chanted, but nevertheless I will repeat it; wealth is honored most of all things by men, and has the greatest influence of anything among men. In pursuit of which I am come, leading hither ten thousand spears: for a nobly-born man in poverty is nothing.   335

CHORUS

And see Eteocles here comes to this mediation; thy business it is, Jocasta, being their mother, to speak words, with which thou shalt reconcile thy children.

ETEOCLES, POLYNICES, JOCASTA, CHORUS

ETEOCLES

Mother, I am present; giving this grace to thee, I have come; what must I do? Let some one begin the conference. Since arranging also around the walls the chariots of the bands, I restrained the city, that I may hear from thee the common terms of reconciliation, for which thou hast permitted this man to come within the walls under sanction of a truce, having persuaded me.   343

JOCASTA

Stay; precipitate haste has not justice; but slow counsels perform most deeds in wisdom. But repress that tierce eye and those blasts of rage; for thou art not looking on the Gorgon's head cut off at the neck, but thou art looking on thy brother who is come to thee. And do thou again, Polynices, turn thy face towards thy brother; for looking at the same point with thine eyes, thou wilt both speak better, and receive his words better. But I wish to give you a wise piece of advice. When a friend is enraged with a man his friend, having met him face to face, let him fix his eyes on his friend's eyes, this only ought he to consider, the end for which he is come, but

to have no recollection of former grievances. Thy words then
first, my son, Polynices; for thou art come leading an army
of Argives, having suffered injustice, as thou sayest; and
may some God be umpire and the reconciler of your strife.

POLYNICES
The speech of truth is simple, and those things which are
just need not wily interpretations; for they have energy
themselves; but the unjust speech, unsound in itself,
requires cunning preparations to gloze it. But I have
previously considered for my father's house, and my own
advantage and that of this man; desiring to escape the curses,
which Oedipus denounced formerly against us, I myself of my
own accord departed from this land, having given him to rule
over his own country for the space of a year, so that I myself
should have the government again, having received it in turn,
and not having come into enmity and bloodshed with this man
to perform some evil deed, and to suffer what is now taking
place. But be having assented to this, and having brought the
Gods to witness his oaths, has performed nothing of what he
promised, but himself holds the regal power and my share of
the palace. And now I am ready, having received my own right,
to send the army away from out of this land, and to regulate
my house, having received it in my turn, and to give it up
again to this man for the same space of time, and neither to
lay my country waste, nor to apply to its towers the means of
ascent by the firmly-fixed ladders. Which, should I not meet
with justice, will I endeavor to put in execution: and I call
the Gods as witnesses of this, that acting in every thing
with justice, I am without justice deprived of my country in
the most unrighteous manner. These individual circumstances,
mother, not having collected together intricacies of
argument, have I declared, but both to the wise and to the
illiterate just, as appears to me.   384

CHORUS
To me indeed, although we have not been brought up
according to the Grecian land, nevertheless to me thou
appearest to speak with judgment.   386

ETEOCLES
If the same thing were judged honorable alike by all, and
at the same time wise, there would not be doubtful strife
among men. But now nothing is similar, nothing the same among
mortals, except in names: but the sense is not the same, for
I, my mother, will speak having kept nothing back; I would
mount to the rising of the stars, and sink beneath the earth,

were I able to perform this, so that I might possess the greatest of the Goddesses, kingly power. This prize then, my mother, I am not willing rather to give up to another, than to preserve for myself. For it implies cowardice in him, whoever having lost the greater share, hath received the less; but in addition to this I feel ashamed, that this man having come with arms, and laying the country waste, should obtain what he wishes; for to Thebes this would be a reproach, if through fear of the Mycenaean spear I should give up my sceptre for this man to hold. But he ought, my mother, to effect a reconciliation, not by arms: for speech does every thing which even the sword of the enemy could do. But if he is desirous of inhabiting this land in any other way, it is in his power; but the other point I will never give up willingly.

When it is in my power to rule, ever to be a slave to him? Wherefore come fire, come sword, yoke thy steeds, fill the plains with chariots, since I will not give up my kingly power to this man. For if one must be unjust, it is most glorious to be unjust concerning empire, but in every thing else one should be just.

CHORUS

It is not right to speak well, where the deeds are not glorious; for this is not honorable, but galling to justice.

JOCASTA

My son, Eteocles, not every ill is added to age, but experience has it in its power to evince more wisdom than youth . Why, my child, dost thou so desirously court ambition, the most baneful of the deities? do not thou; the Goddess is unjust. But she hath entered into many families and happy states and hath come forth again, to the destruction of those who have to do with her. Of whom thou art madly enamored. This is more noble, my son, to honour equality, which ever links friends with friends, and states with states, and allies with allies: for equality is sanctioned by law among men. But the lesser share is ever at enmity with the greater, and straight begins the day of hatred. For equality arranged also among mortals measures, and the divisions of weights, and defined numbers. And the dark eye of night, and the light of the sun, equally walk their annual round, and neither of them being overcome hath envy of the other. Thus the sun and the night are subservient to men, but wilt not thou brook having an equal share of government, and give his share to him? Then where is justice? Why dost thou honour so unboundedly that prosperous injustice, royalty, and think so highly of her? Is the being conspicuous honorable? At least, it is empty honor. Or dost thou desire to labor much, possessing much in thy house? but what is superfluity? It possesses but a name; since a sufficiency indeed to the temperate is abundance. Neither do men enjoy riches as their own, but having the property of the Gods do we cherish them. 437

And when they list, again do they take them away. Come, if I ask thee, having proposed together two measures, whether it is thy wish to reign, or save the city? Wilt thou say, to reign? But should he conquer thee, and the Argive spears overcome the Cadmaean forces, thou wilt behold this city of the Thebans vanquished, thou wilt behold many captive maidens with violence ravished by men your foes. Bitter then to Thebes will be the power which thou seekest to hold; but yet thou art ambitious of it. To thee I say this: but to thee, Polynices, say I, that Adrastus hath conferred an unwise favor on thee; and foolishly hast thou also come to destroy this city. Come, if thou wilt subdue this land (may which never happen), by the Gods, how wilt thou erect trophies of thy spear? And how again wilt thou sacrifice the first-fruits, having conquered thy country? and how wilt thou engrave upon the spoils by the waters of Inachus, "Having laid Thebes in ashes, Polynices consecrated these shields to the Gods?" Never, my son, may it come to thee to receive such glory from the Greeks. But again, shouldest thou be conquered, and should the arms of the other prevail, how wilt thou return to Argos having left behind ten thousand dead? 457

Surely some one. will say, O! unfortunate marriage alliance! O Adrastus, who placed them on us, through the nuptials of one bride we are lost! Thou art hastening two ills, my son, to be deprived of those, and to fail in this. Give up your too great ardor, give it up; the follies of two when they clash together in the same point, are the most hateful ill. 463

CHORUS

O ye Gods, may ye be averters of these ills, and grant to the children of Oedipus some means of agreement.

ETEOCLES

My mother, this is not a contest of words, but intervening time is fruitlessly wasted; and thy earnestness avails nothing; for we shall not agree in any other way, than on the terms proposed, that I holding the sceptre be monarch of this land. Forbearing then tedious admonitions, let me have my way; and do thou begone from out these walls, or thou shalt die. 470

POLYNICES

By whose hand? Who is there so invulnerable, who having pointed the murderous sword against me, shall not bear the same fate?

ETEOCLES

He is near, not far removed from thee: dost thou look on these my hands?

POLYNICES

I see them. But wealth is cowardly, and feeble, loving life.

ETEOCLES

And therefore hast thou come, with such a host against one who is nothing in arms?   475

POLYNICES

For a cautious general is better than one daring.

ETEOCLES

Thou art insolent, having trusted in the truce, which preserves you from death.

POLYNICES

A second time again I demand of you the sceptre and my share of the land.

ETEOCLES

I will admit no demand, for I will regulate my own family.

POLYNICES

Holding more than your share?   480

ETEOCLES

I own it; but quit this land.

POLYNICES

O ye altars of my paternal Gods.

ETEOCLES

Which thou art come to destroy?

POLYNICES

Do ye hear me?   484

                    ETEOCLES
Who will hear thee, who art marching against thy country?

                    POLYNICES
And ye shrines of the Gods delighting in the milk-white
steeds . . .

                    ETEOCLES
Who hate thee.

                    POLYNICES
I am driven out of my own country.

                    ETEOCLES
For thou hast come to destroy it.

                    POLYNICES
With injustice indeed, ye Gods!   490

                    ETEOCLES
At Mycenae call upon the Gods, not here.

                    POLYNICES
Thou art impious.

                    ETEOCLES
But not my country's enemy, as thou art.

                    POLYNICES
Who drives me out without my share.

                    ETEOCLES
And I will put thee to death in addition.   495

                    POLYNICES
My father, hearest thou what I suffer?

                    ETEOCLES
For he hears what wrongs thou doest.

                    POLYNICES
And thou, my mother?

                    ETEOCLES
It is not lawful for thee to mention thy mother.

POLYNICES

O my city!   500

ETEOCLES

To Argos go, and call on Lerna's stream.

POLYNICES

I will go, do not distress thyself; but thee, my mother, I
mention with honor.

ETEOCLES

Depart from out of the country.

POLYNICES

I will go out: but grant me to see my father.

ETEOCLES

You will not obtain your request.   505

POLYNICES

But my virgin sisters then.

ETEOCLES

Never shaft thou behold these.

POLYNICES

O my sisters!

ETEOCLES

Why callest thou on these—being their greatest enemy?

POLYNICES

My mother, but thou farewell.   510

JOCASTA

Do I experience any thing that is well, my son?

POLYNICES

I am no longer thy child.

JOCASTA

To many troubles was I born.

POLYNICES

For he throws insults on us.

ETEOCLES

For I am insulted in turn.   515

POLYNICES

Where wilt thou stand before the towers?

ETEOCLES

Why dost thou ask me this question?

POLYNICES

I will oppose myself to thee, to slay thee.

ETEOCLES

Desire of this seizes me also.

JOCASTA

Wretched me! what will ye do, my children?   520

POLYNICES

The deed itself will shew.

JOCASTA

Will ye not escape your father's curses?

ETEOCLES

Let the whole house perish!

POLYNICES

Since soon my blood-stained sword will not remain any longer in inactivity. But I call to witness the land that nurtured me, and the Gods, how dishonored I am driven from this land, suffering such foul treatment, as a slave and not born of the same father Oedipus. And if any thing befalls thee, my city, blame not me, but him; for against my will have I come, and against my will am I driven from this land. And thou, king Apollo, God of our streets, and ye shrines, farewell, and ye my equals, and ye altars of the Gods receiving the victims; for I know not if it is allowed me ever again to address you. But hope does not yet slumber, in which I have trusted with the favor of the Gods, that having slain this man, I shall be master of this Theban land.   525

ETEOCLES

Depart from out of the country; with truth indeed did your father give you the name of Polynices by some divine foreknowledge, a name corresponding with strife.

CHORUS

Cadmus came from Tyre to this land, before whom the quadrupede heifer bent with willing fall, shewing the accomplishment of the oracle, where the divine word ordered him to colonize the plains of the Aonians productive of wheat, where indeed the fair-flowing stream of the water of Dirce passes over the verdant and deep-furrowed fields, where the [. . . .] mother produced Bacchus, by her marriage with Jove, whom the wreathed ivy twining around him instantly, whilst yet a babe, blest and covered with its verdant shady branches, an event to be celebrated with Bacchic revel by the Theban virgins and inspired women. There was the blood-stained dragon of Mars, the savage guard, watching with far-rolling eyeballs over the flowing fountains and grassy streams; whom Cadmus, having come for water for purification, slew with a fragment of rock, the destroyer of the monster having thrown his arms with blows on his blood-stained head, by the counsel of the divine Pallas born without mother, having thrown the teeth fallen to the earth upon the deep-furrowed plains. Whence the earth sent forth a spectacle, an armed [host] above the extreme limits of the ground; but iron-hearted slaughter again united them with their beloved earth; and sprinkled with blood the ground which shewed them to the serene gales of the air. And thee, sprung of old from our ancestor Io, Epaphus, O progeny of Jove, on thee have I called, have I called in a foreign tongue, with prayers in foreign accent, come, come to this land (thy descendants have founded it), where the two Goddesses Proserpine and the dear Goddess Ceres, queen of all (since earth nurtures all things), have held their possessions, send the fire-bearing Goddesses to defend this land: since every thing is easy to the Gods.

ETEOCLES, CHORUS, MESSENGER

ETEOCLES

Go thou, and bring hither Creon son of Menoeceus, the brother of my mother Jocasta, saying this, that I wish to communicate with him counsels of a private nature and those which concern the common welfare of the country, before we go into battle and the ranks of war. And see, he spares the trouble of your steps, by his presence; for I see him coming towards my palace.   563

CREON, ETEOCLES, CHORUS

CREON
Surely have I visited many places, desiring to see you,
king Eteocles! and I have gone round to the gates and the
guards of the Thebans, seeking you.

ETEOCLES
And indeed I have wished to see you, Creon, for I found
attempts at reconciliation altogether fail when I came and
entered into conference with Polynices.   567

CREON
I have heard that he aspires to higher thoughts than
Thebes, having trusted in his alliance with Adrastus and his
army. But it becomes us to hold these things in dependence on
the Gods. But what is most immediately before us, this am I
come to acquaint you with.   571

ETEOCLES
What is this? for I understand not your speech.

CREON
A prisoner is arrived from the Argives.

ETEOCLES
Does he bring us any news of those stationed there?

CREON
The Argive army is preparing quickly to surround the city
of the Thebans with thickly-ranged arms.   575

ETEOCLES
Therefore must we draw our forces out of the Theban city.

CREON
Whither? Dost thou not in the impetuosity of youth see what
it behooves thee to see?

ETEOCLES
Without these trenches, as we are quickly about to fight

CREON
Small are the forces of this land; but theirs innumerable.

ETEOCLES
I know that they are bold in words.   581

CREON

Argos of the Greeks has some renown.

ETEOCLES

Be confident; quickly will I fill the plain with their slaughter.

CREON

I would it were so: but this I see is a work of much labor.

ETEOCLES

Know that I will not restrain my forces within the walls.

CREON

And yet the whole of victory is prudence.   586

ETEOCLES

Dost thou wish then that I have recourse to other measures?

CREON

To every measure indeed, rather than hazard all on one battle.

ETEOCLES

What if we were to attack them by night from ambush?

CREON

If, having failed, at least you can have a safe retreat hither.   590

ETEOCLES

Night brings the same advantage to all, but more to the daring.

CREON

Dreadful is it to fail in the darkness of night.

ETEOCLES

But shall I lead my force against them while at their meal?

CREON

That would cause terror; but we must conquer.

ETEOCLES

The ford of Dirce is indeed deep to pass.   595

CREON
Every thing is inferior to a good guard.

ETEOCLES
What then, shall I charge the Argive army with my cavalry?

CREON
And there the army is fenced round with chariots.

ETEOCLES
What then shall I do? give up the city to the enemy?

CREON
By no means; but deliberate if thou art wise.   600

ETEOCLES
What more prudent forethought is there?

CREON
They say that they have seven men, as I have heard.

ETEOCLES
What have they been commanded to do? for their strength is
small.

CREON
To head their bands, to besiege the seven gates.   604

ETEOCLES
What then shall we do? I will not wait this indecision.

CREON
Do thou thyself also choose seven men for the gates.

ETEOCLES
To head divisions, or for single combat?

CREON
To head divisions, having selected the bravest.   608

ETEOCLES
I understand you; to guard the approach to the walls.

CREON
And with them other generals; one man sees not every thing?

ETEOCLES
Having chosen them for boldness, or prudence in judgment?

CREON
For both; for one without the other availeth nothing.   612

ETEOCLES
It shall be so: and having gone to the city of the seven towers, I will appoint chiefs at the gates, as you advise, having opposed equal champions against equal foes. But to mention the name of each would be a great delay, the enemy encamped under our very walls. But I will go, that I may not be idle with my hand. And may it befall me to find my brother opposed to me, and being joined with me in battle, to take him with my spear (and to slay him, who came to desolate my county). But it is thy duty to attend to the marriage of my sister Antigone and thy son Haemon, if I fail aught of success; but the firm vow made before I now confirm at my going out. Thou art my mother's brother, why need I use more words? Treat her worthily, both for thine own and my sake. But my father incurs the punishment of the rashness he brought upon himself, having quenched his sight; I praise him not; even us will he put to death with his execrations, should he gain his point. But one thing is left undone by us, if the soothsayer Tiresias have any oracle to deliver, to enquire this of him; but I will send thy son, Creon, Menoeceus, of the same name with thy father, to bring Tiresias hither.

With pleasure will he enter into conversation with you; but I lately reviled him with his divining art, so that he is offended with me. But this charge I give the city with thee, Creon; if my arms should conquer, that the body of Polynices be never buried in this Theban land; but that the man who buries him shall die, although he be a friend. This I have told you: but my attendants I tell, bring out my arms, and my panoply which covers me, that we may go this appointed contest of the spear with victorious justice. But to Caution, the most valued of the Goddesses, will we address our prayers to preserve this city.   642

CHORUS
Mars, cause of infinite woe, why, I pray, art thou so possessed with blood and death, so discordant with the revels of Bacchus? Thou dost not in the circle of beautiful dancers in the bloom of youth, having let flow thy hair, on the breath of the flute modulate strains, in which there is a lovely power to renew the dance. But with thy armed men, having excited the array of Argives against Thebes with blood, thou

dancest before the city in a most inharmonious revel, thou movest not thy foot maddened by the thyrsus clad in fawn-skins, but thy solid-hoofed steed with thy chariot and horses' bits; and bounding at the streams of Ismenus, thou art borne rapidly in the chariot-course, having excited against the race of those sown (by Cadmus,) a raging host that grasp the shield, well armed, adverse to us at the walls of stone: surely discord is some dreadful Goddess, who devised all these calamities against the princes of this land, the Labdacidae involved in woe. O thou forest of heavenly foliage, most productive of beasts, thou snowy eye of Diana, Cithaeron, never oughtest thou to have nourished him doomed to death, the son of Jocasta, Oedipus, the babe who was cast out from his home, marked by the golden clasps. Neither ought that winged virgin the Sphinx, that mountain monster, that grief to this land, to have come, with her most inharmonious lays; who formerly approaching our walls, bore in her four talons the descendants of Cadmus to the inaccessible light of heaven, whom the infernal Pluto sends against the Thebans; but other ill-fated discord among the children of Oedipus springs up in the palace and in the city. For that which is not honorable, never can be honorable, as neither can children the unhallowed offspring of the mother, the pollution of the father. But she came to a kindred bed. Thou didst produce, O (Theban) land! thou didst ⁶⁷³

produce formerly (as I heard the foreign report, I heard it formerly at home), the race sprung from teeth from the fiery-crested dragon fed on beasts, the proudest honour of Thebes.

But to the nuptials of Harmonia the Gods came of old, and by the harp and by the lyre of Amphion uprose the walls of Thebes the tower of the double streams, at the midst of the pass of Dirce, which waters the verdant plain before Ismenus. And To, our ancient mother, doomed to bear horns, brought forth a line of Theban kings. But this city receiving ten thousand goods one in change for another, hath stood in the highest chaplets of war. ⁶⁸³

(TIRESIAS led by his daughter,
MENOECEUS, CREON, CHORUS)

TIRECIAS

Lead onward, my daughter, since thou art an eye to my blind steps, as the star to the mariners. Placing my steps hither on this level plain, proceed lest we stumble; thy father is feeble; and preserve carefully in thy virgin hand my calculations which I took, having learnt the auguries of the birds, sitting in the sacred seats where I foretell the future.   689

My child, Menoeceus, son of Creon, tell me, how far is the remainder of the journey through the city to thy father? Since my knees are weary, and with difficulty I accomplish such a long journey.   692

CREON

Be of good cheer; for thou hast steered thy foot, Tiresias, near to thy friends; but take hold of him, my son. Since every chariot, and the foot of the aged man is used to expect the assistance of another's hand.

TIRECIAS

Well: I am present; but why didst thou call me with such haste, Creon?   695

CREON

We have not as yet forgotten: but recover thy strength, and collect thy breath, having thrown aside the fatigue occasioned by the journey.

TIRECIAS

I am relaxed indeed with toil, brought hither from the Athenians the day before this. For there also was a contest of the spear with Eumolpus, where I made the descendants of Cecrops splendid conquerors. And I wear this golden chaplet, as thou seest, having received the first-fruits of the spoil of the enemy.   702

CREON

Thy victorious garlands I make a happy omen. For we, as thou well knowest, are tossing in a storm of war with the Greeks, and great is the hazard of Thebes. The king Eteocles has therefore gone forth adorned with his armor already to battle with the Argives. But to me has he sent that I might learn from you, by doing what we should be most likely to preserve the city.   708

TIRECIAS

For Eteocles' sake indeed I would have stopped my mouth, and represt the oracles, but to thee, since thou desirest to know them, will I declare them: for this land labors under the malady of old, O Creon, from the time when Laius became the father of children in spite of the Gods, and begat the wretched Oedipus. a husband for his mother. But the cruel lacerations of his eyes were in the wisdom of the Gods, and a warning to Greece. Which things the sons of Oedipus seeking to conceal among themselves by the lapse of time, as about forsooth to escape from the Gods, erred through their ignorance, for they neither giving the honour due to their father, nor allowing him a free liberty, infuriated the unfortunate man: and he breathed out against them dreadful threats, being both in affliction, and moreover dishonored. And I, what things omitting to do, and what words omitting to speak on the subject, have nevertheless fallen into the hatred of the sons of Oedipus? But death from their mutual hands is near them, O Creon. 725

And many corses fallen around corses, having mingled the weapons of Argos and Thebes, shall cause bitter lamentations to the Theban land. And thou, O wretched city, art sapped from thy foundations, unless men will obey my words. For this were the first thing, that not any of the family of Oedipus should be citizens, nor king of the territory, inasmuch as they are possessed by demons, and are they that will overthrow the city. And since the evil triumphs over the good, there is one other thing requisite to ensure preservation. But, as this is neither safe for me to say, and distressing to those on whom the lot has fallen, to give to the city the balm of preservation, I will depart: farewell; for being an individual with many shall I suffer what is about to happen, if it must be so; for what can I do! 738

CREON

Stay here, old man.

TIRECIAS

Lay not hold upon me. 740

CREON

Remain; why dost thou fly me?

TIRECIAS

Thy fortune flies thee, but not I.

CREON

Tell me the means of preserving the citizens and their city.

TIRECIAS

Thou wishest now indeed, and soon thou wilt not wish.

CREON

And how am I not willing to preserve my country? 745

TIRECIAS
Art thou willing then to hear, and art thou eager?

CREON
For towards what ought I to have a greater eagerness?

TIRECIAS
Hear now then my prophecies.—But this first I wish to ascertain clearly, where is Menoeceus who brought me hither.

CREON
He is not far off, but close to thee.   750

TIRECIAS
Let him depart then afar from my oracles.

CREON
He that is my son will keep secret what ought to be kept secret.

TIRECIAS
Art thou willing then that I speak in his presence?

CREON
Yes: for he would be delighted to hear of the means of preservation.   754

TIRECIAS
Hear now then the tenor of my oracles; what things doing ye may preserve the city of the Cadmeans. It is necessary for thee to sacrifice this thy son Menoeceus for the country, since thou thyself callest for this fortune.

CREON
What sayest thou, what word is this thou hast spoken, old man?

TIRECIAS
As circumstances are, thus also oughtest thou to act.

CREON
O thou, that hast said many evils in a short time!   760

TIRECIAS
To thee at least; but to thy country great and salutary.

                              CREON
        I heard not, I attended not; let the city go where it will.

                             TIRECIAS
        This is no longer the same man; he retracts again what he
said.

                              CREON
        Farewell! depart; for I have no need of thy prophecies.

                             TIRECIAS
        Has truth perished, because thou art unfortunate?   765

                              CREON
        By thy knees I implore thee, and by thy reverend locks.

                             TIRECIAS
        Why kneel to me? the evils thou askest are hard to be
controlled.

                              CREON
        Keep it secret; and speak not these words to the city.

                             TIRECIAS
        Dost thou command me to be unjust? I cannot be silent.

                              CREON
        What then wilt thou do to me? Wilt thou slay my son?   770

                             TIRECIAS
        These things will be a care to others; but by me will it
be spoken.

                              CREON
        But from whence has this evil come to me, and to my child?

                             TIRECIAS
        Well dost thou ask me, and comest to the drift of my
discourse. It is necessary that he, stabbed in that cave where
the earth-born dragon lay, the guardian of Dirce's fountain,
give his gory blood a libation to the earth on account of the
ancient wrath of Mars against Cadmus, who avenges the
slaughter of the earth-born dragon; and these things done, ye
shall obtain Mars as your ally. But if the earth receive fruit
in return for fruit, and mortal blood in return for blood, ye
shall have that land propitious, which formerly sent forth a
crop of men from seed armed with golden helmets; but there

must of this race die one, who is the son of the dragon's jaw.
                                                                    783
But thou art left among us of the race of those sown men, pure in thy descent, both by thy mother's side and in the male line; and thy children too: Harmon's marriage however precludes his being slain, for he is not a youth, (for, although he has not approached her bed, he has yet contracted the marriage). But this youth, devoted to this city, by dying may preserve his native country. And he will cause a bitter return to Adrastus and the Argives, casting back death over their eyes, and Thebes will he make illustrious: of these two fates choose the one; either preserve thy child or the state.

Every information from me thou hast:—lead me, my child, towards home;—but whoever exercises the art of divination, is a fool; if indeed he chance to shew disagreeable things, he is rendered hateful to those to whom he may prophesy; but speaking falsely to his employers from motives of pity, he is unjust as touching the Gods.—Phoebus alone should speak in oracles to men, who fears nobody.
                                                                    799

CREON, MENOCEUS, CHORUS

CHORUS
Creon, why art thou mute compressing thy voice in silence, for to me also there is no less consternation.
                                                                    800

CREON
But what can one say?—It is clear however what my answer will be. For never will I go to this degree of calamity, to expose my son a victim for the state. For all men live with an affection towards their children, nor would any give up his own child to die. Let no one praise me for the deed, and slay my children. But I myself, for I am arrived at a mature period of life, am ready to die to liberate my country. But haste, my son, before the whole city hears it, disregarding the intemperate oracles of prophets, fly as quickly as possible, having quitted this land. For he will tell these things to the authorities and chiefs, going to the seven gates, and to the officers: and if indeed we get before him, there is safety for thee, but if thou art too late, we are undone, thou diest.
                                                                    813

MENOECEUS
Whither then fly? To what city? what friends?

                              CREON
    Wheresoever thou wilt be farthest removed from this
country.   815

                            MENOECEUS
    Therefore it is fitting for thee to speak, and for me to
do.

                              CREON
    Having passed through Delphi—

                            MENOECEUS
    Whither is it right for me to go, my father?

                              CREON
    To the land of Aetolia.

                            MENOECEUS
    And from this whither shall I proceed?   820

                              CREON
    To Thesprotia's soil.

                            MENOECEUS
    To the sacred seat of Dodona?

                              CREON
    Thou understandest.

                            MENOECEUS
    What then will there be to protect me?

                              CREON
    The conducting deity.   825

                            MENOECEUS
    But what means of procuring money?

                              CREON
    I will supply gold.

                            MENOECEUS
    Thou sayest well, my father. Go then, for having proceeded
to salute thy sister, whose breast I first sucked, Jocasta I
mean, deprived of my mother, and reft from her, an orphan, I
will depart and save my life. But haste, go, let not thy
purpose be hindered.   831

MENOCEUS, CHORUS

MENOECEUS

Ye females, how well removed I my father's fears, having deceived him with words, in order to gain my wishes; who sends me out of the way, depriving the city of its good fortune, and gives me up to cowardice. And these things are pardonable indeed in an old man, but in my case it deserves no pardon to become the deserter of that country which gave me birth. That ye may know then, I will go, and preserve the city, and will give up my life for this land. For it is a disgraceful thing, that those indeed who are free from the oracle, and are not concerned with any compulsion of the Gods, standing at their shields in battle, shall not be slow to die fighting before the towers for their country; and I, having betrayed my father, and my brother, and my own city, shall depart coward-like from out of the land; but wherever I live, I shall appear vile. No: by that Jove that dwelleth amidst the constellations, and sanguinary Mars, who set up those sown men, who erst sprung from the earth, to be kings of this country. But I will depart, and standing on the summit of the battlements, stabbing myself over the dark deep lair of the dragon, where the prophet appointed, will give liberty to the country—the word has been spoken. But I go, by my death about to give no mean gift to the state, and will rid this land of its affliction. For if every one, seizing what opportunity he had in his power of doing good, would persist in it, and bring it forward for his country's weal, states, experiencing fewer calamities, henceforward might be prosperous.　856

CHORUS

Thou earnest forth, thou earnest forth, O winged monster, production of the earth, and the viper of hell, the ravager of the Cadmeans, big with destruction, big with woes, in form half-virgin, a hostile prodigy, with thy ravening wings, and thy talons that preyed on raw flesh, who erst from Dirce's spot bearing aloft the youths, accompanied by an inharmonious lay, thou broughtest, thou broughtest cruel woes to our country; cruel was he of the Gods, whoever was the author of these things. And the moans of the matrons, and the moans of the virgins, resounded in the house, in a voice, in a strain of misery, they lamented some one thing, some another, in succession through the city. And the groaning and the noise was like to thunder, when the winged virgin bore out of sight any man from the city. But at length came by the mission of the Pythian oracle Oedipus the unhappy to this land of Thebes, to us then indeed delighted, but again came woes. For he, wretched man, having gained the glorious victory over the enigmas, contracts a marriage, an unfortunate marriage with his mother, and pollutes the city.   875

And fresh woes does the unfortunate man cause to succeed with slaughter, devoting by curses his sons to the unhallowed contest.—With admiration, with admiration we look on him, who is gone to kill himself for the sake of his country's land; to Creon indeed having left lamentations, but about to make the seven-towered gates of the land greatly victorious. Thus may we be mothers, thus may we be blest in our children, O dear Pallas, who destroyedst the blood of the dragon by the hurled stone, driving the attention of Cadmus to the action, whence with rapine some fiend of the Gods rushed on this land.

MESSENGER, JOCASTA, CHORUS

MESSENGER

Ho there! who is at the gate of the palace? Open, conduct Jocasta from out of the house.—What ho! again—after a long time indeed, but yet come forth, hear, O renowned wife of Oedipus, ceasing from thy lamentations, and thy tears of grief.   889

JOCASTA

O most dear man, surely thou comest bearing the news of some calamity, of the death of Eteocles, by whose shield thou always didst go, warding off the weapons of the enemy. What new message, I pray, dost thou come to deliver? Is my son dead or alive? Tell me.   893

MESSENGER

He lives, be not alarmed for this, for I will rid thee of this fear.

JOCASTA

But what? In what state are our seven-towered ramparts?

MESSENGER

They stand unshaken, nor is the city destroyed.   895

JOCASTA

Came they in danger from the spear of Argos?

MESSENGER

To the very extreme of danger; but the arms of Thebes came off superior to the Mycenaean spear.

JOCASTA

Tell me one thing, by the Gods, whether thou knowest anything of Polynices (since this is a concern to me also) whether he sees the light.

MESSENGER

Thus far in the day thy pair of children lives.   900

JOCASTA

Be thou blest. But how did ye stationed on the towers drive off the spear of Argos from the gates? Tell me, that I may go and delight the old blind man in the house with the news of his country's being preserved.

MESSENGER

After that the son of Creon, he that died for the land, standing on the summit of the towers, plunged the black-handled sword into his throat, the salvation of this land, thy son placed seven cohorts, and their leaders with them, at the seven gates, guards against the Argive spear; and he drew up the horse ready to support the horse, and the heavy-armed men to reinforce the shield-bearers, so that to the part of the wall which was in danger there might be succor at hand. But from the lofty citadel we view the army of the Argives with their white shields, having quitted Tumessus and now come near the trench, at full speed they reached the city of the land of Cadmus. And the paean and the trumpet? at the same time from them resounded, and off the walls from us. And first indeed Parthenopaeus the son of the huntress (*Atalanta*) led his division horrent with their thick shields against the Neïtan gate, having a family device in the middle of his shield, Atalanta destroying the Aetolian hoar with her distant-wounding bow. And against the Praetan gate marched the prophet Amphiaraüs, having victims in his car, not bearing an insolent emblem, but modestly having his arms without a device. But against the Ogygian gate stood Prince Hippomedon, bearing an emblem in the middle of his shield, the Argus gazing with his spangled eyes, (some eyes indeed with the rising of the stars awake, and some with the setting closed, as we had the opportunity of seeing afterwards when he was dead.) But Tydeus was drawn up at the Homoloïan gate, having on his shield a lion's skin rough with his mane, but in his right hand he bore a torch, as the Titan Prometheus, intent on firing the city. But thy son Polynices drew up his array at the Crenean gate; but the swift Potnian mares, the emblem on his shield, were starting through fright, well circularly grouped within the orb at the handle of the shield, so that they seemed infuriated.   934

But Capaneus, not holding less notions than Mars on the approaching battle, drew up his division against the Electran gate. Upon the iron embossments of his shield was an earth-born giant bearing upon his shoulders a whole city, which he had torn up from the foundations with bars, an intimation to us what our city should suffer. But at the seventh gate was Adrastus, having his shield filled with a hundred vipers, bearing on his left arm a representation of the hydra, the boast of Argos, and from the midst of the walls the dragons were bearing the children of the Thebans in their jaws. But I had the opportunity of seeing each of these, as I took the word of battle to the leaders of the divisions. And first indeed we fought with bows, and javelins, and distant-wounding slings, and fragments of rocks; but when we were conquering in the fight, Tydeus shouted out, and thy son on a sudden, "O sons of the Danaï, why delay we, ere we are galled with their missile weapons, to make a rush at the gates all in a body, light-armed men, horsemen, and those who drive the chariots?" And when they heard the cry, no one was backward; but many fell, their heads besmeared with blood; of us also you might have seen before the walls frequent divers toppling to the ground; and they moistened the parched earth with streams of blood. But the Arcadian, no Argive, the son of Atalanta, as some whirlwind falling on the gates, calls out for fire and a spade, as though he would dig up the city. But Periclymenus the son of the God of the Ocean stopped him in his raging, hurling at his head a stone, a wagon-load, a pinnacle rent from the battlement; and dashed in pieces his head with its auburn hair, and crushed the suture of the bones, and besmeared with blood his lately blooming cheeks; nor shall he carry back his living form to his mother, glorious in her bow, the daughter of Maenalus. But when thy son saw this gate was in a state of safety, he went to another, and I followed.   967

But I see Tydeus, and many armed with shields around him, darting with their Aetolian lances at the highest battlements of the towers, so that our men put to flight quitted the heights of the ramparts; but thy son, as a hunter, collects them together again; and posted them a second time on the towers; and we hasten on to another gate, having relieved the distress in this quarter. But Capaneus, how can I express the measure of his rage! For he came bearing the ranges of a long-reaching ladder, and made this high boast, "That not even the hallowed fire of Jove should hinder him from taking the city from its highest turrets." And these things soon as he had proclaimed, though assailed with stones, he clambered up, having contracted his body under his shield, climbing the slippery footing of the bars of the ladder: but when he was now mounting the battlements of the walls Jupiter strikes him with his thunder; and the earth resounded, insomuch that all trembled; and his limbs were hurled, as it were by a sling, from the ladder separately from one another, his hair to heaven, and his blood to the ground, and his limbs, like the whirling of Ixion on his wheel, were carried round; and his scorched body falls to the earth. But when Adrastus saw that Jove was hostile to his army, he stationed the host of the Argives without the trench. But ours on the contrary, when they saw the auspicious sign from Jove, drove out their chariots, horsemen and heavy-armed, and rushing into the midst of the Argive arms engaged in fight: and there were all the sorts of misery together: they died, they fell from their chariots, and the wheels leaped up and axles upon axles: and corses were heaped together with corses.—We have preserved then our towers from being overthrown to this present day; but whether for the future this land will be prosperous, rests with the Gods.   998

CHORUS

To conquer is glorious; but if the Gods have the better intent, may I be fortunate!

JOCASTA

Well are the ways of the Gods, and of fortune; for my children live, and my country has escaped; but the unhappy Creon seems to feel the effects of my marriage, and of Oedipus's misfortunes, being deprived of his child; for the state indeed, happily, but individually, to his misery: but recount to me again, what after this did my two sons purpose to do?   1005

MESSENGER

Forbear the rest; for in every circumstance hitherto thou art fortunate.

JOCASTA

This hast thou said so as to raise suspicion; I must not forbear.

MESSENGER

Dost thou want any thing more than that thy sons are safe?

JOCASTA
In what follows also I would hear if I am fortunate.

MESSENGER
Let me go: thy son is deprived of his armour-bearer. 1010

JOCASTA
Thou concealest some ill and coverest it in obscurity.

MESSENGER
I cannot speak thy ills after thy happiness.

JOCASTA
But thou shalt, unless fleeing from me thou fleest through
the air.   1013

MESSENGER
Alas! alas! Why dost thou not suffer me to depart after a
message of glad tidings, but forcest me to tell calamities?—
Thy sons are intent on most shameful deeds of boldness—to
engage in single combat apart from the whole army, having
addressed to the Argives and Thebans in common a speech, such
as they never ought to have spoken. But Eteocles began,
standing on the lofty turret, having commanded to proclaim
silence to the army. And he said, "O generals of the Grecian
land, and chieftains of the Danaï, who have come hither, and
O people of Cadmus, neither for the sake of Polynices barter
your lives, nor for my cause. For I myself, taking this danger
on myself, alone will enter the lists with my brother: and if
indeed I slay him, I will dwell in the palace alone; but
should I be subdued, I will give it up to him alone. But you,
ceasing from the combat, O Argives, shall return to your land,
not leaving your lives here; (of the Theban people also there
is enough that lieth dead.") Thus much he spake; but thy son
Polynices rushed from the ranks, and approved his words. But
all the Argives murmured their applause, and the people of
Cadmus, as thinking this plan just. And after this the
generals made a truce, and in the space between the two armies
pledged an oath to abide by it. And now the two sons of the
aged Oedipus clad their bodies in an entire suit of brazen
armor. And their friends adorned them, the champion of this
land indeed the chieftains of the Thebans; and him the
principal men of the Danai. And they stood resplendent, and
they changed not their color, raging to let forth their spears
at each other. But their friends on either side as they passed
by encouraging them with words, thus spoke. "Polynices, it
rests with thee to erect the statue of Jove, emblem of

victory, and to confer a glorious fame onArgos." But to Eteocles on the other hand; "Now thou tightest for the state, now if thou come off victorious, thou art in possession of the sceptre." These things they said exhorting them to the combat. But the seers sacrificed the sheep, and scrutinized the shooting of the flames, and the bursting *of the gall*, the moisture adverse *to the fire*, and the extremity of the flame, which bears a twofold import, both the sign of victory, and the sign of being defeated. But if thou hast any power, or words of wisdom, or the soothing charms of incantation, go, stay thy children from the fearful combat, since great the danger, (and dreadful will be the sequel of the contest, namely, tears for thee, deprived this day of thy two children.)   1056

JOCASTA

O my child, Antigone, come forth from before the palace; the state of thy fortune suits not now the dance, nor the virgin's chamber, but it is thy duty, in conjunction with thy mother, to hinder two excellent men and thy brothers verging towards death from falling by each other's hands.   1060

ANTIGONE, JOCASTA, CHORUS

ANTIGONE

With what new horrors, mother of my being, dost thou call out to thy friends before the house?

JOCASTA

O my daughter, the life of thy brothers is gone from them.

ANTIGONE

How sayest thou?

JOCASTA

They are drawn out in single combat.

ANTIGONE

Alas me! what wilt thou say, my mother?   1065

JOCASTA

Nothing of pleasant import; but follow.

ANTIGONE

Whither? leaving my virgin chamber.

JOCASTA

To the army.

ANTIGONE

I am ashamed to go among the crowd.

JOCASTA

Thy present state admits not bashfulness.   1070

ANTIGONE

But what shall I do then?

JOCASTA

Thou shalt quell the strife of the brothers.

ANTIGONE

Doing what, my mother.

JOCASTA

Falling before them with me.   1074

ANTIGONE

Lead to the space between the armies; we must not delay.

JOCASTA

Haste, daughter, haste, since, if indeed I reach my sons before they engage, I still exist in heaven's fair light, but if they die, I shall lie dead with them.   1077

CHORUS

Alas! alas! shuddering with horror, shuddering is my breast; and through my flesh came pity, pity for the unhappy mother, on account of her two children, whether of them then will distain with blood the other (alas me for my sufferings, Jove, earth), the own brother's neck, the own brother's life, in arms, in slaughter? Wretched, wretched I, over which corse then shall I raise the lamentation for the dead? O earth, earth, the two beasts of prey, bloodthirsty souls, brandishing the spear, will quickly distain with blood the fallen, fallen enemy. Wretches, that they ever came to the thought of a single combat! In a foreign strain will I mourn with tears my elegy of groans due to the dead. Destiny is at hand—death is near; this day will decide the event.   1090

Ill-fated, ill-fated murder because of the Furies! But I see Creon here with clouded brow advancing towards the house, I will cease therefore from the groans I am uttering.

CREON, CHORUS

CREON

Ah me! what shall I do? whether am I to groan in weeping myself, or the city, which a cloud of such magnitude encircles as to cast us amidst the gloom of Acheron? For my son has perished having died for the city, having achieved a glorious name, but to me a name of sorrow. Him having taken just now from the dragon's den, stabbed by his own hand, I wretched bore in my arms; and the whole house resounds with shrieks; but I, myself aged, am come after my aged sister Jocasta, that she may wash and lay out my son now no more. For it behooves the living well to revere the God below by paying honors to the dead.   1103

CHORUS

Thy sister is gone out of the house, O Creon, and the girl Antigone attending the steps of her mother.

CREON

Whither? and for what hap? tell me.

CHORUS

She heard that her sons were about to come to a contest in single battle for the royal palace.

CREON

How sayest thou? whilst I was fondly attending to my son's corse, I arrived not so far in *knowledge*, as to be acquainted with this also.   1109

CHORUS

But thy sister has indeed been gone some time; but I think, Creon, that the contest, in which their lives are at stake, has already been concluded by the sons of Oedipus.

CREON

Ah me! I see indeed this signal, the downcast eye and countenance of the approaching messenger, who will relate every thing that has taken place.   1113

MESSENGER, CREON, CHORUS

MESSENGER

O wretched me! what language or what words can I utter? we are undone—

CREON
Thou beginnest thy speech with no promising prelude. 1115

MESSENGER
Oh wretched me! doubly do I lament, for I hear great calamities.

CREON
In addition to the calamities that have happened dost thou still speak of others?

MESSENGER
Thy sister's sons, O Creon, no longer behold the light.

CREON
Ah! alas! thou utterest great ills to me and to the state.

MESSENGER
O mansions of Oedipus, do ye hear these things of thy children, who have perished by similar fates? 1120

CHORUS
Ay, so that, had they but sense, they would weep.

CREON
O most heavy misery! Oh me wretched with woes! alas! unhappy me!

MESSENGER
If that thou knewest the evils yet in addition to these.

CREON
And how can there be more fatal ills than these? 1125

MESSENGER
Thy sister is dead with her two children.

CHORUS
Raise, raise the cry of woe, and smite your heads with the blows of your white hands.

CREON
Oh unhappy Jocasta, what an end of thy life and of thy marriage hast thou endured in the riddles of the Sphinx! But how took place the slaughter of her two sons, and the combat arising from the curse of Oedipus? tell me. 1130

MESSENGER

The success of the country before the towers indeed thou knowest; for the circuit of the wall is not of such vast extent, but that thou must know all that has taken place. But after that the sons of the aged Oedipus had clad their limbs in brazen armor, they came and stood in the midst of the plain between the two armies, ready for the contest, and the fierceness of the single battle. And having cast a look towards Argos, Polynices uttered his prayer; "O venerable Juno (for I am thine, since in marriage I joined myself with the daughter of Adrastus, and dwell in that land), grant me to slay my brother, and to cover with blood my hostile hand bearing the victory."And Eteocles looking at the temple of Pallas, glorious in her golden shield, prayed; "O Daughter of Jove, grant me with my hand to hurl my victorious spear from this arm home to the breast of my brother, (and slay him who came to lay waste my country.") And when the sound of the Tuscan trumpet was raised, as the torch, the signal for the fierce battle, they sped with dreadful rush towards each other; and like wild boars whetting their savage tusks, they met, their cheeks all moist with foam; and they rushed forward with their lances; but they couched beneath the orbs of their shields, in order that the steel might fall harmless. 1151

But if either perceived the other's eye raised above the verge, he drove the lance at his face, intent to be beforehand with him: but dexterously they shifted their eyes to the open ornaments of their shields, so that the spear was made of none effect. And more sweat trickled down the spectators than the combatants, through the fears of their friends. But Eteocles, stumbling with his foot against a stone, which rolled under his tread, places his limb without the shield. But Polynices ran up with his spear, when he saw a stroke open to his steel, and the Argive spear passed through the shank. And all the host of the Danaï shouted for joy. And the hero who first was wounded, when he perceived his shoulder exposed in this effort, pierced the breast of Polynices with his lance, and gave joy to the citizens of Cadmus, but he broke the point of his spear. But being come to a strait for a spear, he retreated backward on his leg, and taking a stone of marble, he hurled it and crashed his antagonist's spear in the middle: and the battle was on equal terms, both being deprived of the spear in their hands. 1169

Then seizing the handles of their swords they met at close quarters, and, as they clashed their shields together, raised a great tumult of battle around them. And Eteocles having a sort of idea of its success, made use of a Thessalian stratagem, *which he had learned* from his connection with that country. For giving up his present mode of attack, he brings his left foot behind, protecting well the pit of his own stomach; and stepping forward his right leg, he plunged the sword through the navel, and drove it to the vertebra? But the unhappy Polynices bending together his side and his bowels falls weltering in blood. But the other, as he were now the victor, and had subdued him in the fight, casting his sword on the ground, went to spoil him, not fixing his attention on himself, but on that his purpose. Which thing also deceived him; for Polynices, he that fell first, still breathing a little, preserving his sword e'en in his deathly fall, with difficulty indeed, but he did stretch his sword to the heart of Eteocles. And holding the dust in their gripe they both fall near one another, and determined not the victory.

CHORUS

Alas! alas! to what degree, O Oedipus, do I groan for thy misfortunes! but the God seems to have fulfilled thy imprecations. 1189

MESSENGER

Hear now then woes even in addition to these—For when her sons having fallen were breathing their last, at this moment the wretched mother rushes before them, and when she perceived them stricken with mortal wounds she shrieked out, "Oh my sons, I am come too late a succor:" and throwing herself by the side of her children in turn, she wept, she lamented with moans her long anxiety in suckling them *now lost*: and their sister, who accompanied to stand by her in her misery, at the same time *broke forth*; "supporters of my mother's age! Oh ye that have betrayed my hopes of marriage, my dearest brothers!"—But king Eteocles heaving from his breast his gasping breath, heard his mother, and putting out his cold clammy hand, sent not forth indeed a voice; but from his eyes spoke her in tears to signify affection. 1203

But Polynices, who yet breathed, looking at his sister and his aged mother, thus spoke: "We perish, my mother; but I grieve for thee, and for this my sister, and my brother who lies dead, for being my friend, he became my enemy, but still my friend.—But bury me, O mother of my being, and thou my sister, in my native land, and pacify the exasperated city, that I may obtain thus much at least of my country's land, although I have lost the palace. And close my eyelids with thy hand, my mother" (and he places it himself upon his eyes), "and fare ye well! for now darkness surroundeth me." 1212

And both breathed out their lives together. And the mother, when she saw what had taken place, beyond endurance grieving, snatched the sword from the dead body, and perpetrated a deed of horror; for she drove the steel through the middle of her throat, and lies dead on those most dear to her, having each in her arms embraced. But the people rose up hastily to a strife of opinions; we indeed, as holding, that my master was victorious; but they, that the other was; and there was also a contention between the generals, those on the other side contended, that Polynices first struck with the spear, but those on ours that there was no victory where the combatants died. (And in the mean time Antigone withdrew from the army;) but they rushed to arms; but fortunately by a sort of foresight the people of Cadmus had sat upon their shields: and we gained the advantage of falling on the Argives not yet accoutred in their arms.   1227

And no one made a stand, but flying they covered the plain; and immense quantities of blood were spilt of the corses that fell, but when we were victorious in the fight, some indeed raised the image of Jove emblem of victory, but some of us stripping the shields from the Argive corses sent the spoils within the city. But others with Antigone are bearing hither the dead for their friends to lament over. But these contests have in some respect turned out most happy for this state, but in other respect most unhappy.   1235

CHORUS
No longer the misfortunes of the house come to our ears, we may also see before the palace these three fallen corses, who have shared the dark realms by a united death.   1237

(The dead bodies borne.)

ANTIGONE, CREON, CHORUS

ANTIGONE
Not veiling the softness of my cheek on which my ringlets fall, nor caring for the purple glow of virginity under my lids, the blush of my countenance, I am borne along the bacchanal of the dead, rending the fillet from my hair, rejecting the saffron robe of delicateness, having the mournful office of conducting the dead. Alas! alas! woe is me! Oh Polynices, thou well answeredst to thy name! Alas me! Oh Thebes! but thy strife, no strife, but murder consummated with murder, hath destroyed the house of Oedipus with dreadful, with mournful blood. But what groan responsive to my sufferings, or what lament of music shall I invoke to my tears, to my tears, O house, O house, bearing these three

kindred bodies, my mother, and her children, the joy of the fury? who destroyed the entire house of Oedipus, what time intelligently he unfolded the difficult song of the fierce monster, having thereby slain the body of the fierce musical Sphinx.

1253

Alas me! my father; what Grecian, or what Barbarian, or what other of the noble in birth, of mortal blood, in time of old ever bore such manifest sufferings of so many ills? Wretched I, how do I lament! What bird, sitting on the highest boughs of the oak or pine, will sing responsive to my lamentations, who have lost my mother? who weep the strain of grief in addition to these moans *for my brothers*, about to pass my long life in floods of tears.—Which shall I bewail? On which first shall I scatter the first offerings rent from my hair? On my mother's two breasts of milk, or upon the death-wounds of my two brothers?

1263

Alas! alas! Leave thine house, bringing thy sightless eye, aged father, Oedipus, shew thy wretched age, who within thy palace, having poured the gloomy darkness over thine eyes, draggest on a long life. Dost thou hear wandering in the hall,—resting thy aged foot upon the couch in a state of misery?

1268

OEDIPUS, CREON, ANTIGONE, CHORUS

OEDIPUS

Why, O virgin, hast thou with the most doleful tears called me forth leaning on the support of a blind foot to the light, a bed-ridden man from his darksome chamber, grey-headed, an obscure phantom of air—a dead body beneath the earth—a flitting dream?

1272

ANTIGONE

O father, thou shalt receive words of unhappy tidings; no longer do thy children behold the light, nor thy wife, who ever was employed in attending as a staff on thy blind foot, my father: alas me!

1275

OEDIPUS

Alas me, for my sufferings! for well may I groan and vociferate these things. The three souls, tell me, my child, by what fate, how quitted they this light?

ANTIGONE

Not for the sake of reproaching thee, nor exulting over thee, but for grief I speak: thy evil genius, heavy with swords, and fire, and wretched combats, has rushed down upon thy children, O my father.   1280

                              OEDIPUS
Alas me! ah! ah!

                              ANTIGONE
Why dost thou thus groan?

                              OEDIPUS
Alas me! my children!

                              ANTIGONE
Thou wouldest grieve indeed, if looking on the chariot of the sun drawn by its four steeds, thou couldest direct the sight of thine eyes to these bodies of the dead.   1285

                              OEDIPUS
The evil of my sons indeed is manifest; but my wretched wife, by what fate, my child, did she perish?

                              ANTIGONE
Causing to all tears of grief they could not contain, to her children she bared her breast, a suppliant she bared it, holding it up in supplication. But the mother found her children at the Electran gate, in the mead where the lotus abounds, contending with their lances in the common war, as lions bred in the same cave, with the blood-wounds now a cold, a gory libation, which Pluto received, and Mars gave. And having seized the brazen-wrought sword from the dead she plunged it into her flesh, but with grief for her children she fell amidst her children. But all these sufferings, my father, has the God heaped this day upon our house, whoever he be, that adds this consummation.   1298

                              CHORUS
This day hath been the beginning of many woes to the house of Oedipus; but may life be more fortunate!

                              CREON
Now indeed cease from your grief, for it is time to think of the sepulture. But hear these words, Oedipus; Eteocles, thy son, hath given to me the dominion of this land, giving them as a marriage portion to Haemon, and with them the bed of thy daughter Antigone. I therefore will not suffer thee any longer to dwell in this land. For clearly did Tiresias say, that never, whilst thou dost inhabit this land, will the

state be prosperous. But depart; and this I say not from insolence, nor being thine enemy, but on account of thy evil genius, fearing lest the country suffer any harm.   1308

OEDIPUS

O Fate, from the beginning how wretched (and unhappy) didst thou form me, (if ever other man was formed!) whom, even before I came into the light from my mother's womb, when yet unborn Apollo foretold that I should be the murderer of my father Laius, alas! wretch that I am! And when I was born, again my father who gave me life, seeks to take my life, considering that I was born his enemy: for it was fated that he should die by my hands, and he sends me, poor wretch, as I craved the breast, a prey for the wild beasts: where I was preserved—for would that Cithaeron, it ought, had sunk to the bottomless chasms of Tartarus, for that it did not destroy me; but the God fixed it my lot to serve under Polybus my master: but I unhappy man, having slain my own father, ascended the bed of my wretched mother, and begat children, my brothers, whom I destroyed, having received down the curse from Laius, and given it to my sons. For I was not by nature so utterly devoid of understanding, as to have devised such things against my eyes, and against the life of my children, without the interference of some of the Gods. Well!—what then shall I ill-fated do? who will accompany me the guide of my dark steps? She that lies here dead! living, well know I, she would. But my noble pair of sons? I have no sons.—But still in my vigor can I myself procure my sustenance? Whence?—Why, Creon, dost thou thus utterly kill me? for kill me thou wilt, if thou shalt cast me out of the land. Yet will I not appear base, stretching my hands around thy knees, for I cannot belie my former nobleness, not even though my plight is miserable.

CREON

Well has it been spoken by thee, that thou wilt not touch my knees, but I cannot permit thee to dwell in the land. But of these corses, the one we must even now bear to the house; but the body of Polynices cast out unburied beyond the borders of this land. And these things shall be proclaimed to all the Thebans: "whoever shall be found either crowning the corse, or covering it with earth, shall receive death for his offence." But thou, ceasing from the groans for the three dead, retire, Antigone, within the house, and behave as beseems a virgin, expecting the approaching day in which the bed of Haemon awaits thee.   1345

ANTIGONE

Oh father, in what a state of woes do we miserable beings lie! How do I lament for thee! more than for the dead! For it is not that one of thy ills is heavy, and the other not heavy, but thou art in all things unhappy, my father.—But thee I ask, our new lord, (wherefore dost thou insult my father here, banishing him from his country?) Why make thy laws against an unhappy corse?   1351

CREON

The determination of Eteocles this, not mine.

ANTIGONE

It is absurd, and thou a fool to enforce it.

CREON

How so? Is it not just to execute injunctions?   1354

ANTIGONE

No, if they are base, at least, and spoken with ill intent.

CREON

What! will he not with justice be given to the dogs?

ANTIGONE

No, for thus do ye not demand of him lawful justice.

CREON

We do; since he was the enemy of the state, who least ought to be an enemy.

ANTIGONE

Hath he not paid then his life to fortune?   1359

CREON

And in his burial too let him now satisfy vengeance. 1360

ANTIGONE

What outrage having committed, if he came after his share of the kingdom?

CREON

This man, that you may know once for all, shall be unburied.

ANTIGONE

I will bury him; even though the city forbid it.

CREON
Thyself then wilt thou at the same time bury near the corse.   1364

ANTIGONE
But that is a glorious thing, for two friends to lie near.

CREON
Lay hold of her, and bear her to the house.

ANTIGONE
By no means—for I will not let go this body.

CREON
The God has decreed it, virgin, not as thou wilt.

ANTIGONE
And this too is decreed—that the dead be not insulted.

CREON
Around him none shall place the moist dust.   1370

ANTIGONE
Nay, by his mother here Jocasta, I entreat thee, Creon.

CREON
Thou laborest in vain, for thou canst not obtain this.

ANTIGONE
But suffer thou me at any rate to bathe the body.

CREON
This would be one of the things forbidden by the state.

ANTIGONE
But let me put bandages round his cruel wounds.   1375

CREON
In no way shalt thou shew respect to this corse.

ANTIGONE
Oh most dear, but I will at least kiss thy lips.

CREON
Thou shalt not prepare calamity against thy wedding by thy lamentations.

ANTIGONE
What! while I live shall I ever marry thy son?

CREON
There is strong necessity for thee, for by what means wilt
thou escape the marriage?   1380

ANTIGONE
That night then shall find me one of the Danaïdae.

CREON
Dost mark with what audacity she hath insulted us?

ANTIGONE
The steel be witness, and the sword, by which I swear.

CREON
But why art thou so eager to get rid of this marriage?

ANTIGONE
I will take my flight with my most wretched father here.

CREON
There is nobleness in thee; but there is some decree of
folly.   1386

ANTIGONE
And I will die with him too, that thou mayest farther know.

CREON
Go—thou shalt not slay my son—quit the land.

OEDIPUS, ANTIGONE, CHORUS

OEDIPUS
O daughter, I praise thee indeed, for thy zealous
intentions.

ANTIGONE
But if I were to marry, and thou suffer banishment alone,
my father?   1390

OEDIPUS
Stay and be happy; I will bear with content mine own ills.

ANTIGONE
And who will minister to thee, blind as thou art, my father?

OEDIPUS
Falling wherever it shall be my fate, I will lie on the ground.

ANTIGONE
But Oedipus, where is he? and the renowned Enigmas?

OEDIPUS
Perished! one day blest me, and one day destroyed.   1395

ANTIGONE
Ought not I then to have a share in thy woes?

OEDIPUS
To a daughter exile with a blind father is shameful.

ANTIGONE
Not to a right-minded one however, but honorable, my father.

OEDIPUS
Lead me now onward, that I may touch thy mother.

ANTIGONE
There: touch the aged woman with thy most dear hand. 1400

OEDIPUS
O mother! Oh most hapless wife!

ANTIGONE
She doth lie miserable, having all ills at once on her.

OEDIPUS
But where is the fallen body of Eteocles, and of Polynices?

ANTIGONE
They lie extended before thee near one another.

OEDIPUS
Place my blind hand upon their unhappy faces.   1405

ANTIGONE
There: touch thy dead children with thy hand.

OEDIPUS
O ye dear wrecks, unhappy, of an unhappy father.

ANTIGONE
O name of Polynices, most dear indeed to me.

OEDIPUS
Now, my child, is the oracle of Apollo come to pass.

ANTIGONE
What? but dost thou mention evils in addition to these
evils?   1410

OEDIPUS
That I must die an exile at Athens.

ANTIGONE
Where? what citadel of Attica will receive thee?

OEDIPUS
The sacred Colonus, and the temple of the Equestrian God.
But stay—minister to thy blind father here, since thou art
desirous of sharing his exile.   1414

ANTIGONE
Go to thy wretched banishment: stretch forth thy dear hand,
aged father, having me as thy guide, as the gale that wafts
the ship.   1416

OEDIPUS
Behold, I go, my child, be thou my unhappy conductor.

ANTIGONE
We are, we are indeed unhappy above all Theban virgins.

OEDIPUS
Where shall I place my aged footstep? Bring my staff, my
child.

ANTIGONE
This way, this way come; here, here place thy foot, thou
that hast the strength of a dream.   1420

OEDIPUS
Alas! alas! for my most wretched flight!—To drive me, old
as I am, from my country—Alas! alas! the dreadful, dreadful
things that I have suffered!

ANTIGONE
What suffered! what suffered! Vengeance sees not the
wicked, nor repays the foolishness of mortals.   1424

OEDIPUS
That man am I, who mounted aloft to the victorious heavenly
song, having solved the dark enigma of the virgin Sphinx.

ANTIGONE
Dost thou bring up again the glory of the Sphinx?
Forbear from speaking of thy former successes. These
wretched sufferings awaited thee, father, being an exile from
thy country to die any where. Leaving with my dear virgins
tears for my loss, I depart far from my country, wandering in
state not like a virgin's.   1430

OEDIPUS
Oh! the excellency of thy mind!

ANTIGONE
In the calamities of a father at least it will make me
glorious. Wretched am I, on account of the insults offered to
thee and to my brother, who has perished from the family, a
corse denied sepulture, unhappy, whom, even if I must die, my
father, I will cover with secret earth.   1435

OEDIPUS
Go, shew thyself to thy companions.

ANTIGONE
They have enough of my lamentations.

OEDIPUS
But make thy supplications at the altars.

ANTIGONE
They have a satiety of my woes.

OEDIPUS
Go then, where stands the fane of Bacchus unapproached, on
the mountains of the Maenades.   1440

ANTIGONE
To whom I formerly, clad in the skin of the Theban fawn,
danced the sacred step of Semele on the mountains, conferring
a thankless favor on the Gods?

OEDIPUS
O ye inhabitants of my illustrious country, behold, I, this Oedipus, who alone stayed the violence of the bloodthirsty Sphinx, now, dishonored, forsaken, miserable, am banished from the land. Yet why do I bewail these things, and lament in vain? For the necessity of fate proceeding from the Gods a mortal must endure.

CREON
(O greatly glorious Victory, mayest thou uphold my life, and cease not from crowning me!)   1448

                         (Exit.)

                         (LIGHTS FADE.)

                         (CURTAINS.)

                         (END OF PLAY.)